The
Adolescent
Parent

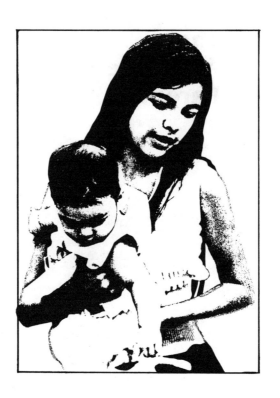

The Adolescent Parent

by
Nicholas J. Anastasiow, Ph.D.
Professor, Special Education
Hunter College

with
Mary Anastasiow, Ph.D.
Cindy Carlson, M.S.
Carol J. Garrett, M.A.
Charles Granger, Ph.D.
Richard Lehrer, M.S.
Allan Shwedel, Ph.D.

·P·A·U·L·H·
BROOKES
PUBLISHING C⁰

Baltimore • London

Paul H. Brookes Publishing Co.
Post Office Box 10624
Baltimore, Maryland 21204

Typeset by The Composing Room of Michigan, Inc. (Grand Rapids)
Manufactured in the United States of America by
Universal Lithographers, Inc. (Cockeysville, Maryland)

Permission to reprint the following material is gratefully acknowledged:

Pages 50–57: Excerpts from Werner, Emmy E., et al., *The Children of Kauai*, pp.
77–78, 80–81. Honolulu: The University Press of Hawaii. Copyright 1971 by
University of Hawaii Press.

Library of Congress Cataloging in Publication Data

Anastasiow, Nicholas J.
    The adolescent parent.

    Bibliography: p.
    Includes index.
    1. Adolescent parents—Addresses, essays, lectures. 2. Child
development—Addresses, essays, lectures. I. Anastasiow, Mary,
1952–   . II. Title.
HQ759.64.A5   362.7′96   81-18190
ISBN 0-933716-25-7   AACR2

Contents

Chapter **8**
> **Integrating Community-Level Services for Pregnant**
> **Adolescents and Adolescent Parents**

Chapter **9**
> **How FEED Operates in Different Communities**

Chapter **10**
> **The Problem Recognized—Solutions in Dispute**

Contributors

Mary Anastasiow, Ph.D.
Department of Educational Psychology
  and Statistics
State University of New York
1400 Washington Avenue
Albany, New York 12222

Nicholas J. Anastasiow, Ph.D.
Professor, Special Education
Hunter College
440 East 26th Street
New York, New York 10010

Cindy Carlson, M.S.
Department of Educational Psychology
Indiana University
Bloomington, Indiana 47401

Carol J. Garrett, M.A.
State of Colorado
Department of Institutions
Division of Youth Services
Planning and Evaluation
4255 South Knox Court
Denver, Colorado 80236

Charles Granger, Ph.D.
Kettle Moraine Hospital
Oconomowoc, WI 53066

Richard Lehrer, M.S.
Department of Educational Psychology
  and Statistics
State University of New York
1400 Washington Avenue
Albany, New York 12222

Allan Shwedel, Ph.D.
Institute for Child Behavior and
  Development
University of Illinois
Champaign, Illinois 61820

Preface

THE PROBLEM of preteen and teenage pregnancy is, for many perplexing reasons, without a solution. The issue is perhaps most appropriately perceived as composed of a complex set of factors; each is addressed in turn by the authors of this book. The chapters represent a "logic chain," which, in its entirety, promotes a broader understanding of the forces and issues surrounding adolescent pregnancy as well as speaks to a potential solution.

The major premise of this book is that preteens and teenagers who bear infants are likely to do so in environments that place the mother and infant at risk. Both mother and infant may suffer from the birth process, and either or both may die or become handicapped. Those young women who survive are likely to continue life at the poverty level and become enmeshed in a series of defeating relationships that will find the young mother with a second child within one year and, very possibly, four or five more children before she is beyond childbearing age. The children of these adolescents are likely to be of low birth weight or to suffer perinatal stress and, following the stress, are likely to decline progressively, due to the mothers' lack of knowledge of how to facilitate their infants' development. To wit, the world over, more and more infants are being born who by school age may be classified as handicapped.

The authors of this volume believe that even if teenage pregnancies continue, this trend toward an increasing number of handicapped children can be arrested. First, knowledge of how to facilitate an infant's development is well established. Second, and as a related factor, although a great number of the young men and women who potentially will be teen parents are ignorant of child growth and development and of how to responsibly facilitate it (these young people are likely, in the main, to reside in the lower class and use the outmoded childrearing practices of their parents, which are negatively correlated with IQ and language development), we believe an extensive experience with children and a course in child development can help them learn about and care for normal and handicapped children. We believe the responsibility for providing such an experience must be one shared by community agencies—medical, social, and educational.

This book is the argument for such programs. Chapter 1 places the pregnancy problem as manifested in the United States in a world context and places the pregnancy issue in a context of sexuality and family values. Chapter 2 explores the developmental issues of adolescence. Chapter 3 looks at adolescent parents, their knowledge base, and life chances. Chapter 4 sets forth the findings that demonstrate why parenting practices are so critical for development. Chapter 5 speculates as to why the early years are so critical for intellectual development and summarizes the findings of the most recent intervention projects. Chapter 6 describes programs designed to work with adolescent parents, as well as child development programs for preteens and teenagers before they become parents. Chapter 7 analyzes the data supporting the effectiveness of those programs. Chapter 8 presents ways and means of engaging community agencies in working together. Chapter 9 discusses specific means of implementing a child development curriculum in school. Chapter 10 reviews current efforts to deal with the pregnancy issue on the national level and suggests directions for those efforts.

Most of the authors have been associated with Project FEED (Facilitative Environments Encouraging Development), originally funded by the Bureau of Education for the Handicapped (now Special Education Programs), formerly directed by Dr. Edwin W. Martin. Jane DeWeerd was the main support officer for the project for the 6 years of funding. When we needed help, we were always able to depend on Ms. DeWeerd and Dr. Martin. The project has operated in urban, rural, and suburban communities in Maine, New Hampshire, New York, Indiana, Kentucky, Illinois, Texas, Oregon, California, Hawaii, Israel, and the Philippines. The Educational Development Corporation now distributes the program's *Implementation and Curriculum Guide* (see Chapter 9) at cost and will provide the names of former field coordinators who can help establish a program in interested communities. Drs. Susan Eklund, Sadie Grimmett, and Gerald Smith of Indiana University have all served as directors of the project, and our efforts owe thanks to them, as well as to Drs. Tom O'Shaughnessy of State University College, Potsdam, New York, Patricia Eggleston of Orange Coast College, and Dominic Gullo of Kent State.

Acknowledgments

A NUMBER OF PEOPLE have contributed to the development of this work. Roberta Parry Anastasiow did much to improve the text by her careful editing and critical review. Arthur Stengel did the same, reading and critiquing chapters. Kathleen Greenwalt deciphered original drafts, rewrites and rewritten rewrites, and incomplete bibliographical entries. I owe them all. Also, thanks to Emmy Elizabeth Werner who encouraged me to gather together our experiences into this book.

For my teenage mother—
Tilitha Robinett Anastasiow

The
Adolescent
Parent

1

Adolescent Pregnancy
World Perspective

Nicholas J. Anastasiow

ADOLESCENT PREGNANCY IS not a new phenomenon. There have been adolescent parents for generations, and in some cultures, as noted later in this chapter, early marriage and pregnancy are encouraged. In the United States, it is not uncommon for high school graduates to marry and have their first child while still in their teens. Indeed, this appears to be a well-established and accepted pattern for marriage and childbearing throughout the world. Thus, 18- or 19-year-olds who bear children are not of major concern in this book.

What is of concern is the large number of women 16 years of age and under who are becoming pregnant, many of whom bear infants that are premature and of low birth weight. The majority of these young women are and remain unmarried, and face a life of isolation, welfare, and low socioeconomic status. The future of these mothers is bleak; they appear to be victims of a complex set of physiological and societal factors that are beyond their control. It is these factors that the authors of this text address.

The following section addresses the worldwide occurrence of teenage pregnancy, the forces contributing to the problem, and the efforts being made to respond to the increased number of very young, unmarried teenage mothers and the high-risk infants born to them. The conditions that confront those mothers and infants in the United States are in serious need of remediation. The section below also examines programs that have been designed to reduce the number of teenage pregnancies as well as programs designed to help the young mother cope with those conditions.

1

Adolescent pregnancies are a product of both sexuality and social values and practices. Where adolescent pregnancy is socially acceptable, the issue is moot. If however, it is neither desired nor highly valued by a society, then some socially acceptable means of coping with the issue must be brought to bear. There exists a wide range of responses to sexuality, including the denying or ignoring of its existence; some cultures have strong, punitive responses to out-of-wedlock sexual activity. Sexual intercourse is a product of physiological sexual maturity and sexuality interacting with social values. Both factors have undergone marked changes in most cultures. Let us examine the physiological changes first.

CONTRIBUTING FACTORS

Earlier Physiological Maturation

Both female and male sexes are reaching physiological maturation at earlier ages than in past generations.

Boys are reaching sexual maturation at a mean age of 12.5 years (Anastasiow, Everett, O'Shaughnessy, Eggleston, & Eklund, 1978). Data indicate that initial nocturnal emissions occur at an average age of 12.2 years (Eskin, 1977). Data from past generations indicate that since the time of Johann Sebastian Bach, there has been about a 4.5-year lowering in the age for voice drop in boys from age 17.5 to 13.5 (Roche, 1979). Voice drop occurs late in the puberty cycles of boys, with increased size in testes, penis growth, and testes descension all preceding it. Of particular importance is that at the initial stage of puberty, boys begin to produce semen and are potentially fertile (Short, 1978). Short refers to boys during this period as "fertile eunuchs," because they produce semen even though they have not yet developed the secondary characteristics of facial hair and enlarged testes.

Girls are now experiencing menses at the mean age of 12.5 years (Cutright, 1972a). This mean age represents about a 2-year drop from the 1900 generation, when the mean was 14.2 years (Tanner, 1968). Yet, menses is but one factor that indicates sexual maturity in girls. Breast development appears a more preferred measure by some researchers, and there are some rare cases in which a girl has become pregnant without having experienced menses (Brown, Harrison, & Smith, 1978). That the mean age for the onset of menses is 12.5 years, with a range of 3 years on each side of the mean, suggests that some girls experience first menses as early as 8 and some as late as 14 or 15 years of age. This is in contrast with past generations, when the mean age for menses onset was 14.5 years and that for early menses was 12.5 years. In general, ovulation occurs about 2 years after first menses. If the age of first menses is 8 years, ovulation, and thus fertility, can occur by age 10 (Cutright, 1972a). It is clear that girls are now capable of conceiving at least 2 years earlier than their grandmothers were.

These female physiological changes are affected by social class differences. Higher social classes tend to experience maturation earlier, while rural and lower socioeconomic classes reach physiological maturity as much as 1 to 2 years later (Short, 1978). Class differences for boys have not been reported.

Given that boys mature at the average age of 12.5 years and girls have first menses at approximately the same age, both sexes are sexually mature before they enter their teens. Thus, the genetic push to engage in sexual activity occurs during the time that young people leave elementary school and enter junior high school. But, the presence of steroids that activate the hypothalamus and pituitary and thus lead to physical maturity and sexuality does not necessarily mean the young person understands the relationship between sexuality, sexual intercourse, and birth or is aware of the responsibilities of childbearing. Brown et al. (1978) raise the crucial question:

> What are we going to do with our sexuality if we acquire the physical capability of reproducing, together with the biological urge to reproduce, many years in advance of the intellectual maturity to handle our sexuality? This is the whole problem of teenage pregnancy (p. 61).

Sexuality as a dominant human trait should not be minimized. Sexuality is firmly based in the genetic code and ensures the survival of the species evolutionarily. LaBarre (1954) has postulated that the sexual drive may be stronger in males than in females. A difference in strength of drive is unimportant here, however. What is of import is the well-established fact that, in either sex, physical sexual maturity is accompanied by a strong urge to engage in sexual activity.

Whereas, on the average, sexual maturity occurs earlier (around age 12), the area of the brain known to be associated with the inhibition or modulation of such desires as sex and aggression does not mature fully until 14 to 15 years of age. It appears that the frontal lobe, particularly the poles or the front third of the lobe, which deals with the control or allocation of the sexual drive, is not completely myelinated until 14 or 15 years of age. Myelin usually signals the full maturation of a brain structure. Further, the frontal lobe area is known to be related to abstract reasoning, anticipation, planning, and processes associated with the self or ego. These processes are hallmarks of adult functioning and are not normally mature until the late adolescent period.

The point is that although sexual maturation is occurring earlier than in past generations, the capacity for sexual behavioral control is not, and therefore the two systems that had previously been coordinated are now out of sync.

It appears that the sexually mature systems are activating drives that cannot be adequately controlled by immature brains. In the absence of societal controls, which are usually imposed by the family, sexually mature young adolescents are particularly susceptible to expressing their sexual impulses.

Earlier Sexuality

It is generally agreed that the 1920s were a time of sexual revolution in Western cultures. Denial of sexual pleasure was rejected as a moral standard by a large portion of such populations (Bolton, 1980). These changes came about due to Western industrialization and the breakdown of rigid moral standards usually labeled as "Victorian values." Since that time, a growing number of persons in Western cultures have participated in sexual intercourse before marriage (Kinsey, Pomeroy, Martin, & Gebhard, 1953). In the 1960s, adolescents in large numbers refused to deny themselves sexual gratification before marriage (Cutright, 1972b).

Figures vary, but Dryfoos (1978) has reported that at least 55% of *all* unmarried 19-year-olds in the United States report that they have engaged in sexual intercourse. Dryfoos suggests that premarital intercourse has actually become the norm. Zelnick and Kantner (1980) have reported that 55% of adolescent women have experienced coitus by age 19, and that 80% of adolescent brides have had premarital sexual intercourse. At younger ages, 18% of boys and 6% of girls have had sexual intercourse by age 13. One-half of males 15 to 17 years old and one-third of their female age peers are sexually active (Alan Guttmacher Institute, 1981). Other studies have reported percentages that range from 65% to 94% for teenage boys experiencing coitus by the age of 18; inner-city figures are higher for both boys and girls of all races and ethnic groups studied (Diepold, 1976). Some studies suggest that many inner-city boys are sexually active at age 12.

Considering the earlier physical maturation and the increased sexual activity of teenagers, the increase in teenage pregnancy rates is understandable.

Pregnancy Rates

An estimated 1.1 million women under the age of 20 became pregnant in the United States during 1978. Of these pregnancies, 554,500 resulted in live births (Alan Guttmacher Institute, 1981). These figures are comparable to the British, who also report 1.1 million pregnancies to women under 20 in 1978. In both countries, although the overall birthrate for mothers of all ages has declined, the number of teen pregnancies and births has increased. Other world data reflect similar trends. In Barbados, Guatemala, El Salvador, the Dominican Republic, and Costa Rica, teen births account for more than half of the live births (Engstrom, 1978).

The United States teenage birthrate was 52 per 1,000 teenage girls in 1978. Higher rates are reported for Thailand, Czechoslovakia, East Germany, Yugoslavia, Rumania, Hungary, and Bulgaria. The latter three have rates over 70 per 1,000. In countries like Japan, where massive campaigns have been conducted to encourage contraceptive use and abortion, the teen birthrate is a very low 3 per 1,000 teenage girls.

Table 1. Total births by state, 1977

States	Under 15 years	15–19 years	All ages	Percentage born to teens (%)
Alabama	405	13,963	61,970	23
Alaska	18	1,117	8,370	14
Arizona	100	7,114	41,848	17
Arkansas	263	8,440	35,737	24
California	861	52,856	347,817	15
Colorado	62	6,324	43,075	15
Connecticut	104	4,293	36,658	12
Delaware	60	1,557	8,630	19
D.C.	96	2,202	10,044	23
Florida	740	22,234	110,922	21
Georgia	574	18,184	84,566	22
Hawaii	20	2,122	16,917	13
Idaho	32	2,706	18,875	15
Illinois	603	29,362	177,393	17
Indiana	275	16,051	85,198	19
Iowa	63	6,241	44,945	14
Kansas	66	6,145	36,944	17
Kentucky	243	12,765	58,655	22
Louisiana	431	16,537	75,017	23
Maine	34	2,657	16,147	17
Maryland	229	9,105	55,832	17
Massachusetts	86	7,755	67,973	12
Michigan	428	22,628	138,473	17
Minnesota	59	7,048	60,251	12
Mississippi	440	11,390	45,485	26
Missouri	247	13,162	73,171	18
Montana	21	1,988	13,315	15
Nebraska	35	3,250	25,209	13
Nevada	29	1,722	10,191	17
New Hampshire	7	1,490	12,096	12
New Jersey	268	11,948	94,112	13
New Mexico	54	4,438	23,066	19
New York	585	30,214	240,258	13
North Carolina	432	17,786	84,598	22
North Dakota	9	1,514	11,421	13
Ohio	455	27,446	161,708	17
Oklahoma	147	9,594	45,457	21
Oregon	69	5,318	37,519	14
Pennsylvania	395	23,492	153,709	16
Rhode Island	17	1,606	11,624	14
South Carolina	312	10,629	49,916	22
South Dakota	22	1,798	12,039	15
Tennessee	380	14,197	66,773	22
Texas	1,061	44,614	229,194	20
Utah	40	4,285	37,880	11

continued

Table 3. (*continued*)

States	Under 15 years	15–19 years	All ages	Percentage born to teens (%)
Vermont	8	935	7,024	13
Virginia	285	12,535	74,294	17
Washington	94	7,586	57,237	13
West Virginia	81	6,419	30,111	22
Wisconsin	103	9,022	68,607	13
Wyoming	7	1,370	8,291	17

Source: Alexander, S. J., Williams, C. D., and Forbush, J. B. 1980. Overview of State Policies Related to Adolescent Parenthood. National Association of State Boards of Education, Washington, D.C.

In the United States, there were 11,455 live births to girls under age 15 out of the 1977 total of 559,154 births to teenage women (Bureau of Vital Statistics, 1977). The racial split between black and white indicates a somewhat higher rate for blacks. From 1973 to 1978, the number of teenage girls becoming pregnant each year increased by 10%–11% (Alan Guttmacher Institute, 1981).

A large number of second and third children are born to young teenagers. As many as 1,545 second children were born to 15-year-olds in 1978, and 5,874 were born to 16-year-olds. A total of 102,419 second children were born to 15- to 19-year-olds (Alan Guttmacher Institute, 1981). The rates are fairly consistent by state. Table 1 presents a breakdown of teenage births by state compared to the overall birthrate in each state in 1977. The percentages range from 11% in Utah to a high of 26% in Mississippi (Bureau of Vital Statistics, 1977).

Cultural Changes

By and large, the urbanized cultures of the world have witnessed a breakdown of the extended family (Parkes, Short, Potts, & Herbertson, 1978). In underdeveloped countries, the values and codes of the family are being lost through migration of the young into urban centers (Farmaian, 1978). Traditionally, the family has been the institution of the culture that has maintained control over teenage sexuality. In the past, the cohesiveness of the family was fairly effective in enforcing and maintaining cultural value systems. With the breakdown of the family, no major institution or force has emerged in the urban cultures to enforce old cultural value systems. Thus, in the absence of the effective enforcement, new values have emerged by fiat. The situation is further compounded by the prevalence of the mass media, which have introduced into the home values that may be alternative to those held by the family.

Television and movies present a neo-romanticized view of sexuality, marriage, and parenthood. Old values and norms have been replaced by new, more lenient values. Families have both less control and less support, particularly in large urban areas, which tend to have a disorganizing effect on them (Chilman, 1978; Ross & Sawhill, 1975).

RESPONSES

Health care personnel may be concerned about births to young teenagers in general. Traditionally, however, most societies have been unconcerned about the young girl who is *married* and becomes pregnant. Generally, there are three distinct, but interrelated, societal orientations toward dealing with teenage pregnancy. First, the one sponsored particularly by family planners encourages contraception to prevent pregnancy. Second, a few cultures, such as those of China and Japan, place great pressure toward sexual abstinence. And, finally, in many cultures where it is the shame of pregnancy out of wedlock that is seen as the problem, early marriage is often encouraged as the best means of controlling illegitimacy (Deschamps & Valantin, 1978).

Marriage

Moslems, Islamics, and Asians represent cultures that have encouraged early marriage. Parents in Moslem countries arrange their daughters' marriages before first menstruation and thereby avoid out-of-wedlock pregnancy. Paxman (1978) has suggested that less than 4% of pregnancies are out of wedlock. In most Moslem countries, 50% of the 15- to 19-year-old women are married; in Egypt, 31%; in Pakistan, 73%; and in India, 70% (Paxman, 1978). Thus, social marriage occurs in the early teens, biological marriage in the later teens.

Early marriage is encouraged as well in Bulgaria, especially among the Tzigase (Gypsy) people, and in many of the developing African countries (Sai, 1978). Of all females age 15 to 19 in Africa, 40% are married or are encouraged to be married soon after first menses. In contrast, marriage rates for 15- to 19-year-old women are lower in Europe, at 7%; in the Soviet Union, at 9%; in Oceania, at 14%; and in the Americas, at 15%.

The legal age for marriage varies among European countries, with restrictions on contraception seemingly prescribed for a respectively younger age. In Spain, the legal age is 12; in Austria, Greece, Hungary, and Portugal, it is 14. As one would imagine, marriage age is not directly tied to fertility rates in all the countries studied. Yet, fertility rates in countries that allow abortions, such as Czechoslovakia, are surprisingly high (Deschamps & Valantin, 1978). The picture of responses to pregnancy is not clear-cut. Italy's legal age of marriage is 18, yet data from 1973 indicate that there were 1,942 marriages among 10- to 14-year-olds and 83,628 marriages among 15- to 19-year-olds. Thus, an older legal age does not seem to prevent early marriage and/or pregnancy.

In the United States, only 34% of the 582,000 live births to 15- to 19-year-olds were to married women. Of the married group, 39% of the infants were conceived before marriage. The marriage rate increased from 13.1 to 19.5 for the 15- to 17-year-olds in 1978, an increase of 64% (Dryfoos, 1978).

The data presented above suggest that if there is pressure to solve the illegitimacy rate by marriage, the solution does not appear to be working. The increase in out-of-wedlock births appears to be the result of an increase in sexual activity at younger ages (10- to 14-year-olds) rather than of increased conception in 15- to 19-year-olds (Dryfoos, 1978). Marriage of 10- to 12-year-olds appears as but a limited solution to the problem of early childbearing, although some cases have been reported (Anastasiow, in press).

Abstinence

Few countries are successful in encouraging sexual abstinence. China, however, has a very low teenage pregnancy rate, with abstinence strongly encouraged and marriage delayed, on the average, until the male is in his late 20s and the female her mid-20s. In Japan, intense constraints are placed on sexual activity for females. In Latin America, strong religious values against premarital sex aid in reducing out-of-wedlock pregnancies. If a girl becomes pregnant, there is great pressure on the parents to see to it that she is married.

The mean age for first sexual intercourse in Sweden and Yugoslavia is a surprising 17 years (Deschamps & Valantin, 1978); thus, some pressure toward abstinence must be operating. The breakdown of abstinence in the Western world has contributed significantly to the enormous increase in teenage pregnancy. In the United States, few voices outside organized religion speak out for abstinence, a situation which at least one leader in the movement decries (Shriver, 1981).

Modified Abstinence

Some countries traditionally have attempted to separate males from females until marriage. Spain, Italy, and certain Moslem countries serve as examples. These societies frequently condone a double standard for males, particularly middle- and upper-class males, allowing them to be sexually active with prostitutes or servants and, in some cases, ignoring adolescent male homosexuality. And, these "traditional" societies are harsh on out-of-wedlock pregnancies. Many pregnant but unmarried women in Egypt are killed by family members who believe the family has been shamed (The Longest Revolution, 1980). These so-called honor killings occur even if the girl has been a victim of rape. The same is true in other Moslem countries, such as Afghanistan. In Egypt, Sudan, Somalia, Kenya, and Indonesia, female circumcision is used to suppress female adolescent sexuality. In addition, early marriage is encouraged in those countries. Double standards of morality exist in Asia, as well. Where agrarian, peasant-based societies are able to exercise sufficient adult control to reduce the problem, it is in the urban areas of most world societies that the out-of-wedlock adolescent pregnancies tend to occur.

Few countries punish the male, particularly if he later marries the girl. As stated, many countries exert great pressure for marriage once pregnancy occurs. In Zambia, however, if the two adolescents involved do not marry, the man is held responsible and can be fined, and the girl is expelled from school. In North Africa, the male may be prosecuted and even jailed if he does not marry the girl. Jail terms of 15 years' compulsory labor may be handed out to older males and of 10 years to men under 20.

Contraception

Some countries, such as Spain and Argentina, prohibit the manufacture and sale of contraceptives (Paxman, 1978). Others, such as China and Sweden, make it mandatory for pharmacies to have contraceptives available (Paxman, 1978). Planned Parenthood programs have encouraged the worldwide distribution of contraceptives and have been largely successful in their distributions.

Practices for distributing contraceptives vary widely across the world. In West Germany and Nigeria, over 70% of the population live in rural areas where neither doctor nor pharmacy is available; yet, the law requires that contraceptives be distributed only through physicians or pharmacies (Paxman, 1978). In Indonesia, Malaysia, the Philippines, and Taiwan, only married couples may buy contraceptives (Paxman, 1978).

In such a diverse, pluralistic country as the United States, it is difficult to state that there is one attitude toward out-of-wedlock childbirth. The push generally, however, is toward contraceptive use rather than early marriage. In the United States, 1 million teenage women visited Family Planning centers for contraceptive information in 1975. Of them, 34% selected the pill for use (Dryfoos, 1978). Laws that have limited the availability of contraceptives to young teens in New York and Massachusetts have been struck down (Paxman, 1978).

Contraceptives are not used by the very young teenager and are more effective with the over-15-year-old. Further, young 10- to 12-year-olds may not have the cognitive awareness to relate the sexual act to "real" childbirth (Anastasiow, 1982).

Abortion and Sterilization

In the review of many professionals, abortion is not a solution, but a response to the problem of adolescent pregnancy. Abortion, however, is on the rise worldwide as a means of controlling birthrates (Paxman, 1978). Abortion is allowed in most eastern and northern European countries as well as in most of the United States. Abortion policies are well established in Czechoslovakia, Hungary, England, Wales, Sweden, and Denmark. Data from Sweden indicate that abortions have so increased as to reduce the overall birthrate from 1971 to 1975 by 20% (Deschamps & Valantin, 1978, p. 107). In Singapore, abortion among teenagers has increased 10-fold in the years 1971 to 1976 (Paxman, 1978, p. 197).

Wide differences exist among countries regarding abortion. Abortion is illegal in many predominantly Catholic countries, such as Spain and Latin America. In the Philippines, it is a criminal offense (Paxman, 1978). Paxman (1978) presents an excellent summary of the wide set of exceptions and rules concerning abortions and teenage pregnancies, which is too complex to discuss here. While there are vocal objections to abortion as a solution to teenage pregnancy in the United States, particularly by members of the Catholic Church, nevertheless, it appears a widely accepted practice. The United States' abortion rate doubled from 1973 to 1979, reaching a total of 1.5 million; in 1979, abortion was the response to adolescent pregnancy for more than 434,000 teenage women. (See Dempsey, 1981, for a recent review of abortion policies in the United States.)

Sterilization is rarely seen as a solution to teenage sexuality (Paxman, 1978). In fact, widespread sterilization of older adults is not in practice. Paxman (1978) has written that in such countries as Chad, India, Bali, Nepal, Niger, Bangladesh, Pakistan, and Tanzania, where 70% of females are married early and have three children by age 21, sterilization could be a solution for limiting additional children (p. 197). However, data are sketchy on voluntary sterilization worldwide. In some countries, such as Saudi Arabia, male and female sterilization is prohibited under Moslem law (Paxman, 1978).

SUMMARY

Societies react and provide solutions to adolescent sexuality in a variety of ways, but, for most, marriage is the only acceptable religious and/or moral solution. Marriage in Western cultures did not attain the status of a sacrament until the late 1700s, when both adult and child deaths diminished, thereby lending stability to both marriage and childrearing (Stone, 1977).

Many cultures, such as the Sinhalese Buddhists, have idealized virginity and the marriage ceremony from ancient times, however. Marriage is a family and cultural event that binds the fabric of society. Births out of wedlock are a threat to that fabric. It is the opinion here that the unity of urban life has been shattered, and teenage sexuality is but one symptom.

The concern in this text is both for the offspring of adolescents and for efforts to enhance the social conditions of these children's and their parents' lives. Later chapters in this book examine the conditions into which the majority of such children are born, as well as those educational and intervention programs that have been designed to enhance their quality of and chances for life.

REFERENCES

Alan Guttmacher Institute, 1981. Teenage Pregnancy: The Problem That Hasn't Gone Away. Alan Guttmacher Institute, New York.

Alexander, S. J., Williams, C. D., and Forbush, J. B. 1980. Overview of State Policies Related to Adolescent Parenthood. National Boards of Education, Washington, D.C.

Anastasiow, N. J. 1982. Preparing adolescents in childrearing: Before and after pregnancy. In: M. Sugar (ed.), Adolescent Parenthood. Spectrum Pub. Inc., Jamaica, N.Y.

Anastasiow, N. J., Everett, M., O'Shaughnessy, T., Eggleston, P. J., and Eklund, S. J. 1978. Improving teenage attitudes towards children, child handicaps, and hospital settings. American Journal of Orthopsychiatry 48(4):663–672.

Bolton, F. G., Jr. 1980. The Pregnant Adolescent: Problems of Premature Parenthood. Sage Publications, Beverly Hills, Calif.

Brown, J. B., Harrison, P., and Smith, M. A. 1978. Oestrogen and pregnanediol excretion through childhood, menarche, and first ovulation. In: A. S. Parkes, R. V. Short, M. Potts, and M. A. Herbertson (eds.), Fertility in Adolescence, pp. 43–64. Galton Foundation, Cambridge, England.

Bureau of Vital Statistics. 1977. Monthly Vital Statistics Report, Advance Report, Final Natality Statistics, Vol. 27, No. 11 (DHEW Publication No. (PHS) 79-1120. Suppl., February 5, 1979.

Chilman, C. 1978. Adolescent Sexuality in a Changing American Society. Social and Psychological Perspectives, U.S. Department of Health, Education, and Welfare, Washington, D.C.

Cutright, P. 1972a. Illegitimacy in the United States, 1920–1968. In: C. F. Westoff and R. Parke, Jr. (eds.), Demographic and Social Aspects of Population Growth, pp. 375–438. U.S. Government Printing Office, Washington, D.C.

Cutright, P. 1972b. The teenage sexual revolution and the myth of an abstinent past. Family Planning Perspectives 4(1):24–31.

Dempsey, J. J. 1981. The Family and Public Policy: The Issue of the 1980s. Paul H. Brookes Publishing Co., Baltimore.

Deschamps, J. P., and Valantin, G. 1978. Pregnancy in adolescence: Incidence and outcome in European countries. In: A. S. Parkes, R. V. Short, M. Potts, and M. A. Herbertson (eds.), Fertility in Adolescence, pp. 101–116. Galton Foundation, Cambridge, England.

Diepold, J. H., Jr. 1976. Adolescent sexual behavior: A review of taboo (1943–1976). Paper presented at Henry Smith Research Conference, Indiana University, Bloomington, Ind., February.

Dryfoos, J. G. 1978. The incidence and outcome of adolescent pregnancy in the United States. In: A. S. Parkes, R. V. Short, M. Potts, and M. A. Herbertson (eds.), Fertility in Adolescence, pp. 85–99. Galton Foundation, Cambridge, England.

Engstrom, L. 1978. Teenage pregnancy in developing countries. In: A. S. Parkes, R. V. Short, M. Potts, and M. A. Herbertson (eds.), Fertility in Adolescence, pp. 117–128. Galton Foundation, Cambridge, England.

Eskin, B. A. 1977. When do nocturnal emissions begin in adolescence? Does that date coincide with or resemble first menstruation in girls? Medical Tribune, February, New York.

Farmaian, S. F. 1978. Socio-cultural aspects of age at marriage in the Middle East. In: A. S. Parkes, R. V. Short, M. Potts, and M. A. Herbertson (eds.), Fertility in Adolescence, pp. 215–226. Galton Foundation, Cambridge, England.

Gardner, H. 1975. The Shattered Mind. Alfred A. Knopf, New York.

Kinsey, A., Pomeroy, W., Martin, C. E., and Gebhard, P. 1953. Sexual Behavior in the Human Female. Saunders Press, Philadelphia.

LaBarre, W. 1954. The Human Animal. University of Chicago Press, Chicago.

The Longest Revolution. 1981. The Center for Women's Studies and Services, P.O. Box 350, San Diego, Calif., Suppl., p. 1.

Parkes, A. S., Short, R. V., Potts, M., and Herbertson, M. A. (eds.). 1978. Fertility in Adolescence. Galton Foundation, Cambridge, England.

Paxman, J. M. 1978. Law, policy, and adolescent sexuality. In: A. S. Parkes, R. V. Short, M. Potts, and M. A. Herbertson (eds.), Fertility in Adolescence, pp. 187–213. Galton Foundation, Cambridge, England.

Roche, A. F. 1979. Secular Trends in Human Growth, Maturation, and Development. Monographs of the Society for Research in Child Development 44(3–4).

Ross, H., and Sawhill, I. V. 1975. Time of Transition. The Urban Institute, Washington, D.C.

Sai, F. A. 1978. Social and psychosexual problems of African adolescents. In: A. S. Parkes, R. V. Short, M. Potts, and M. A. Herbertson (eds.), Fertility in Adolescence, pp. 235–247. Galton Foundation, Cambridge, England.

Short, R. V. 1978. Closing of workshop. In: A. S. Parkes, R. V. Short, M. Potts, and M. A. Herbertson (eds.), Fertility in Adolescence, pp. 248–254. Galton Foundation, Cambridge, England.

Shriver, E. K. 1981. Sex values for teens. The New York Times, March 1.

Stone, L. 1977. The Family, Sex, and Marriage in England, 1500–1800. Harper & Row, New York.

Tanner, J. M. 1968. Earlier maturation in man. Scientific American 218(1):21–27.

Zelnick, M., and Kantner, J. F. 1980. Sexual activity, contraceptive use, and pregnancy among metropolitan area teenagers, 1971–1979. Family Planning Perspectives 12:230.

2

Adolescent Development
Systems and Their Interactions

Mary Anastasiow and Richard Lehrer

THE INTENT of this chapter is to expand understanding of the issue of adolescent pregnancy and parenthood by discussing the various dimensions that make up this complex phenomenon. These dimensions include physiological, psychological, and social developmental components, which occur within a large environmental context, that of family, peers, and culture. To use the knowledge of these specific elements of adolescent growth and development to clarify the issue of adolescent pregnancy, the authors apply a systems approach.

In this context, *systems* refers to a set of interrelated events, among which a distinction is made between the elements of the system and their organization, and the elements outside the system, called the "surround." The three systems of behavior commonly examined in most discussions of adolescence are physical, cognitive, and social development. However, boundaries between these systems are apt to be imprecisely defined. The context within which an adolescent becomes a parent is at once social, physical, and cognitive. Parenting is a social role, the adoption of which necessarily includes sexual maturation as well as those cognitive processes that are involved in the integration of the parent and peer social roles. Adolescent pregnancy and parenthood is best viewed as the interaction of systems—which involves

---

Alphabetical listing of authors indicates equal contribution.

the self-regulation of behavior at physical, cognitive, and social levels of integration.

Before elaborating how developmental components interact to lead to adolescent pregnancy, the chapter focuses attention on how adolescents regulate their behavior within each of these separate domains. The following section describes the sequence of physical and sexual maturation, which is regulated by a cyclic process of hormonal activation. Subsequent sections discuss the cognitive and social domains of adolescent behavior, where self-regulation occurs at more conscious levels. The final section presents a family systems view of adolescent parenthood as reflective of the interaction between sociocultural and individual systems of organization which provide a useful framework for intervention.

PHYSICAL DEVELOPMENT

A hallmark of the adolescent period is the acceleration of physical growth and development of primary and secondary sex characteristics. The first menstrual period, or menarche, usually occurs after the peak in the height growth spurt but does not represent the attainment of full reproductive functioning. Frequently, there is a period of adolescent sterility of about 12 to 18 months after menarche. Early menstrual cycles are irregular and often without ovulation. The average age for menarche in the United States is approximately 12.6 years, and slightly over 13 years of age for girls in most European countries (Bullough, 1981).

There is evidence that the age of onset of menarche fluctuates according to environmental, historical, or cohort variation. Malmquest (1978) has contended that menarche is occurring earlier in economically privileged groups because of better nutrition. Some researchers have compared the current average age of onset with that in the previous century: a comparison of 1830 and 1960 appears to show a lowering of age of about 4 months (Tanner, 1962); others have estimated the comparable difference of 3.6 months (Zacharias & Wurtman, 1969). Frisch and Revelli (1970) have compared differences in rate data during the 20th century and suggested that the secular trend described by Tanner shows evidence of deceleration and may have begun to stop. However, Bullough (1981), in criticism of Tanner, has cited evidence that the data reflecting measurements of menarche during the 1980s were overestimates of the age for onset. He suggests that such age is much lower than that reported by Tanner (1962) and may not reflect a secular trend. Bullough (1981) has cited literary references and marriage laws that document the onset of puberty during the 19th century as occurring between 12 and 14 years of age; he states that "undoubtedly there has been some drop in menarcheal age in the United States since the 19th century to under 13 in the 1980s" (p. 366). In most

European cultures at present, however, the age of menarche is still over 13, so that generalization of European data to American culture, as in Tanner's (1962) sample, may not be valid.

The physiological events that lead to physical maturation and reproductive capacity are in response to brain-triggered hormonal activation. An adolescent may have reproductive capacity prior to fully developed physical maturation because of the interactions among different hormones that control these events. Although for the young adolescent, this apparent asynchrony in visible signs of maturation may cause concern, fluctuations within and between individuals with respect to various aspects of maturity reflect the normal process of maturation.

The regulation of physical growth and development is the result of a cycle of hormonal stimulation that can be best characterized as a negative feedback loop. Negative feedback acts much like a thermostat to regulate the secretion of hormones. This feedback loop comprises specialized cells that are differentially sensitive to certain releaser and activator hormones. For example, the sensor hormones of the hypothalamus have a threshold of sensitivity analogous to that of a thermostat, which determines the levels of hormones in the blood. The threshold of the sensors can be altered by the brain, as happens in puberty. Before puberty, the sensor for estrogen is set so that it responds by discontinuing the release of the follicle-stimulating hormone (FSH) when it (estrogen) is still at relatively low levels in the blood. At puberty, impulses arrive that disinhibit or lower the sensitivity of sensor cells, so that the threshold is raised and cells respond to higher levels of estrogen. The FSH is not switched off as estrogen levels rise, which results in breast and uterus development.

Difference Between Males and Females

The spurt in the skeletal and muscular dimensions are also closely related to the development of the reproductive system. The typical girl is shorter at all ages than the typical boy—except at adolescence. At that time, a major change in the rate of growth occurs, called the circumpuberal, or adolescent, growth spurt. For a year or more, the rate of growth is approximately double that of previous childhood years, or about 7 to 12 cm per year for boys and 6 to 11 cm per year for girls. Females begin their growth spurt approximately 2 years earlier than males, or at age 10½ as contrasted with age 12 for males. This faster maturation of females is also present at birth and continues into late adolescence in most areas of development. Boys surpass females in height at age 14. Girls and boys reach their peak velocity of growth at approximately ages 12 and 14, respectively, and the maximum peak for boys is slightly higher.

Sexual dimorphism is also seen in the differences in body size and shape. Boys have greater breadth through the shoulders, while girls have a proportionate widening of the hips. The differences between males and females attained at final adult height are partially due to the time when the growth spurt began. Boys begin their spurt later but are taller than girls are when it begins. That tempo of growth is also responsible for boys having longer legs.

Thus, considerable changes in hormone secretion occur at puberty. These changes are determined genetically and guided by the brain. Sensors from the brain begin the cycle of sexual maturation. They provide input to the neurological system and organize hormonal secretion that results in changes in physical development. Indeed, all physiological development may be characterized in a similar fashion, that is, wherein system elements interact in a cyclic feedback process of self-regulation. The physical changes that accompany the development of the reproductive function result from internal system interactions and provide input to psychological and social behavioral systems.

The timing—although not the ultimate attainment—of these developmental components is sensitive to environmental influence. Thus, although some changes in sequence may occur and although there is slightly more variation in timing of events than there is in sequence, nevertheless, in human physiological development, there is little variation in the sequence and timing of developmental events. The regulation of growth is controlled through what Waddington (1957) has described as the "canalization of genetic input." Genes that are highly canalized are minimally affected by environmental influence. Genes that control sequence of sexual maturation are more highly canalized (i.e., less environmentally influenced) than are those that determine timing. Further, Tanner (1962) has proposed a notion of self-stabilizing, or target-seeking, genes that modulate the trajectory of growth toward a given, predetermined path of development. Homeoresis, or the maintenance of a flowing and developing process, further regulates the different aspects of growth (Waddington, 1957).

Early and Late Maturers

Given the complexity of physiological components underlying the process of physical and sexual maturation, there is surprisingly limited variation among adolescents in their development. Yet, of course, from the perspective of the individual adolescent, the variation among aspects of one's own development as well as between one and one's peers is a major source of concern. Such is the nature of systems interaction, where biological changes have both a psychological and a sociocultural impact upon behavior. In considering sexual maturity as the product of systems interaction, what is most important is not the sequence but, rather, the time of occurrence of development. Thus, precocity and retardation have great implications for other (behavioral) aspects of development. Studies of early and late maturers alike have shown correlations between their behavior and the way they are perceived by peers and adults.

Early-maturing males tend to report better self-concepts and be more popular, outgoing, aggressive and, as may be expected, more successful in heterosexual relationships than their late-maturing peers (Jones, 1965; Mussen & Jones, 1957). Peers report that, in contrast to early maturers, late maturers are talkative, attention-seeking, restless, and lacking in confidence. However, longitudinal studies that have taken adult follow-up measures of early and late maturers have found late maturers more independent, outgoing, and explorative than their early-maturing peers (Peskin, 1967, 1973). In addition, late maturers were found, as adults, more intellectually curious, more adaptive, and less submissive than early maturers. Peskin (1973) has suggested that early maturers are more advantaged in terms of social development, but that late maturers have the advantage with respect to intellectual control. Similarly, Clausen (1975) has suggested that the late maturer's success is found, not in physical development, but, rather, in intellectual pursuits.

The differences between early- and late-maturing females are less consistent. There is evidence to suggest that females follow certain patterns similar to those of males, with late-maturing women being less advantaged. The impact of social and cultural influences, which has been documented in the more recent studies, indicates that cohort differences and historical effects confound much of the results of comparisons across maturational levels. For example, Nesselroade and Baltes (1974) have found that measures of personality, attitudinal, and achievement variables taken between 1970 and 1972 represented changes across all age groups and not just among adolescents, so that "change in personality traits occurred from 1970 to 1972 because the socialization context for adolescents changed during this period" (p. 59).

There is also a small correlation between physical maturity and cognitive development as evidenced in age-graded exams of achievement. Faster-maturing children tend to have a slight cognitive advantage over children less developmentally advanced. Maccoby (1963) has found that girls have a more rapid and earlier intellectual start than boys in verbal skills, reading, and the ability to count. During the middle school years, boys catch up with girls, and more differences emerge, with boys showing superior mathematical and spatial ability (Bradway & Thompson, 1962). Additionally, there is evidence that abilities as measured by IQ tests continue to grow throughout life and are related to environmental stimulation (Green, 1969; Kangas & Bradway, 1971; Schaie & Gribbin, 1975). Differences between adult males and females in intellectual abilities, therefore, cannot be attributed solely to physiological differences.

Differences in the onset of sexual and physical maturation in males and females influence the social relationships of early adolescence. Early-maturing females are often at a particular disadvantage when they are the first of their peers to show signs of physical and sexual maturity. As young persons' bodies develop, peers and adults begin to respond to them with a new set of expectations of behavior. As described in Chapter 1, there is a strong tendency to engage in sexual activity once physical maturity has been attained. Although the physical and cognitive systems are developing in a parallel fashion, their development is not necessarily congruent. For those adolescents whose sexual growth precedes cognitive maturity, problems are likely to occur, specifically, unwanted adolescent pregnancy. Studies of peer, teacher, and other adult attitudes have indicated that all three groups have increased expectations for sexually mature adolescents in both cognitive and social performance—a pressure that may encourage further development in those areas but that may also demand a level of maturity the adolescent may not be capable of. The section below discusses self-regulation in cognitive and social development in the areas of sexuality, pregnancy, and parenting.

COGNITIVE DEVELOPMENT

Many of the stereotypical characteristics and experiences attributed to adolescents, such as "storm and stress" (Hall, 1904), identity crisis (Erikson, 1968), alienation (Keniston, 1960), and excessive idealization (Inhelder & Piaget, 1958), are testimonies to the recognition of adolescence as a distinct phase in the life cycle. Parenthetically, it should be noted that such a recognition has been anything but precipitous; rather, "adolescence" is almost exclusively a 20th century phenomenon (Aries, 1962). To facilitate understanding of the cognitive aspects of adolescent parenting, it is useful to first compare adolescent development with earlier periods of growth and then examine the implications of adolescent experiences with reference to principles of self-regulation.

Development and Self-Regulation

"Development" is a construct used to describe continuity and change in the organization of an individual's behavior over time. The central feature of a cognitive-developmental approach toward behavior is the position that it is the individual who acts to transform inputs (Neisser, 1967) and, by implication, to construct his or her own reality, rather than merely importing stimuli. For example, the meaning of pregnancy is the result of the individual's transformations of a variety of inputs, including perceptions offered by parents and peers. In this framework, then, cognitive development represents continuity and change in that *organization* through which, over time, the individual acts to transform inputs.

The process of construction is regulated by the individual's attempts to maintain a coherent organization or equilibrium in the relationship between self and sensory inputs. When attention is directed toward elements of the surround, stimuli are analyzed and categorized according to the individual's preexisting organization. More specifically, current inputs are matched up with a previously developed standard, and subsequent behavior is altered to conform more closely to this standard (Carver, 1979). For example, seeing a mirror might lead an individual to decide that his or her hair is in disarray, and subsequent behavior might be directed toward more strictly adhering to that person's existing standard for "neat hair." This matching process is an example of negative feedback control (Powers, 1973), as discussed above. But that principle is now used to describe, not hormones and their interactions, but the interaction among elements of the individual's cognitive system. Although the organizational characteristics of standards undergo a series of transitions during development, the focus here is on the implications that changes in those standards have for behavior, rather than on the mechanisms of developmental change.

Metaphorically, standards result from an individual's effort to construct a well-organized "story" about self; what changes during development are the central themes and overall complexity with which the "character" enacts plots and resolves conflict (Mancuso & Sarbin, in press; Sarbin, 1977). As Averill (1980) explains:

> An analogy with drama may illustrate. A drama is not simply a set of individual roles intertwined in a certain fashion. The drama also has a plot and a plot is different (but not more) than the sum of individual roles. In order to perform a role adequately an actor must not only know his own part, and the parts of others, but he must also understand how various roles relate to the plot and subplots of the play. In the case of social roles the plot is the cultural system (p. 314).

An individual's failure to use contraception during sexual intercourse, for instance, may be due to the absence of planning of sexual activity in the "romantic" story enacted during the course of many adolescent relationships. In addition, the use of contraception requires an anticipation of the future enactment of the "sexually active" role, which may be perceived as incongruent with a previously enacted role of "good girl" (the standard). Furthermore, unanticipated pregnancy might be construed by the participants as more congruent with an ideal, "spontaneous" relationship than would either planned pregnancy or birth control. This example demonstrates the hierarchical nature of cognitive systems, in that the use of contraception is embedded within the larger drama of "love," just as many stories have minor characters and subplots that are subordinate to the major theme and plot. In other words, some standards are more important than others within an individual's cognitive system.

Conversely, when two standards are equally important yet, at the same time, incongruent, the individual becomes "anxious" (Powers, 1973). For example, if Sally loves both Joe and John, but in "different ways," and must for some reason make a choice between them, then in picking Joe, she fails to match to the standard, John, and vice versa. In this situation, we could expect

Sally to exhibit oscillation in behavior—now it's John, then it's Joe; no, it's John—because as Sally attempts to modify her perceptions of her behavior to more closely match up with the standard of John, she simultaneously weakens the match with Joe, and vice versa. To resolve the paradox, Sally must eventually construct a standard of "love" that will subsume both her previous standards. Similarly, an adolescent's decision, or lack thereof, to become pregnant may reflect momentary points in an oscillation between two competing standards or stories for "love." The first story, "romantic love," might demand the abandonment of contraception, whereas a second, "pragmatic love," might also demand the abandonment of contraception, if her partner is a millionaire.

From the developmental point of view, the experience of romantic love may be seen as a benchmark for other, related qualities of adolescent thought, which together constitute a coherent organization, or stage, in the life cycle. The term *stage* refers to the description of a diverse set of individual behaviors that presumably are guided by a relatively smaller set of operating principles (Piaget, 1970). Accordingly, the present discussion of cognitive development during adolescence focuses on general changes in the way individuals organize their worlds. Furthermore, from a systemic viewpoint, these organizational changes increase the individual's ability to predict events and allow him or her to subsume or understand a greater range of phenomena. In short, the individual becomes a better storyteller.

Thought and Experience in Adolescence

Inhelder and Piaget (1958) have attempted to account for intellectual growth during adolescence in terms of changes in underlying logical structures. They contend that the acquisition of formal operations, a particular type of logical structure, is the foremost accomplishment of adolescence. Although this chapter eschews a comprehensive treatment of the acquisition of logical structures, several consequences of that transitional developmental accomplishment should be noted.

First, the adolescent is capable of combinatorial logic and can think about problems that have several variables operating simultaneously. For example, most adolescents can easily generate all possible combinations of four differently colored poker chips or, at a less mundane level, are capable of playing a good hand of poker. One consequence of the ability to reason combinatorially, however, is that the adolescent now sees a host of alternatives, and decision-making may become a problem.

Often, the issue in adolescence is not that the adolescent is incapable of constructing alternative ways of thinking about a problem but, instead, that he or she has difficulty making a choice. Several changes in a typical adolescent's approach toward decision-making occur during the transition from early to late adolescence. Such changes include increases in the consideration of risks and concern for future consequences, the solicitation of the advice of independent specialists, and a cautious attitude toward the vested interests of adult professionals (Lewis, 1981). In view of the developmental transitions in decision-making, the focus of adolescent counseling may, in addition to presenting "sound advice," require emphasis on the acquisition of decision-making skills. In addition, justifications for parental decisions involving their adolescent children must become more complex, as the adolescent now sees many alternatives to such decisions and directives (Elkind, 1967).

A second change in adolescent intellect is the emerging ability to think about thinking, without reference to the concrete world of everyday reality with its implicit spatial and temporal bounds. For example, an adolescent can evaluate the tautologous statement "Either the chip in my hand is green or it is not green" without having to look at the chip as a younger child would (Flavell, 1977). In terms of self-regulation, the adolescent is able to anticipate the future with greater precision than is a younger child. This is done primarily by conducting internal simulations of events (Chi, 1978) as they might occur, not as they have occurred. Inhelder and Piaget (1958) have succinctly characterized this type of anticipation as making reality secondary to possibility, wherein an adolescent's organization of thought leads to the generation of multiple hypotheses for which personal "experiments" are conducted to verify or discard some or all of them. In other words, an adolescent attempts to establish a coherent story, not only in relation to "what is going on now," but also with respect to "what might happen next." The emphasis on the hypothetical is helpful in counseling adolescents, because the counselor can construct scenarios and produce a variety of dramas in coordination with the adolescent. A co-production of drama allows the adolescent to verify that more than one way of enacting any role must necessarily exist. With the help of the counselor, the adolescent can choose that way to express him- or herself which seems the most useful in extending the range of his or her skills.

One immediate consequence of thinking about thought is the construction of ideals. For example, adolescent love may include not only a judgment of the qualities of the other person but also a comparison of such qualities with those of an ideal partner. More important, as adolescents are able to take their own thought as an object, they become capable of introspection and of constructing an imaginary audience for which they perform (Elkind, 1967). The concern of many adolescents for the latest style in apparel, evident in an excursion to a shopping mall, can be viewed as a manifestation of playing to an audience. Thus, young adolescents are relatively more self-conscious than are children or adults (Elkind & Bower, 1979). In addition, many adolescents undertake regimes of self-improvement to reduce the discrepancy between their perceptions of their actions and their perceptions of those of an "ideal" self.

Some Limitations of Adolescent Thinking

Since adolescence appears to be marked by the emergence of a variety of new behavioral skills, particularly an increased ability to forecast the consequences of decisions, one might ask, "Why do adolescents become parents?" On the positive side, it can be noted that assuming an adult role is made possible not only by sexual maturation but also by the adolescent's ability to envision and integrate the complexities of the adult role of parent. However, the decision, or lack thereof, to become a parent often reflects some of the limitations of adolescent thinking. Adolescents often lack the ability to integrate principles with practical reality or actual behavior (Elkind, 1967; Inhelder & Piaget, 1958). Flavell (1963) has described the problem as "a kind of naive idealism, bent on intemperate proposals for reforming and reshaping reality coupled with a cavalier disregard for the practical obstacles which . . . face proposals" (p. 224). In other words, adolescents may fail to see the seed of veracity (and humor) in the aphorism "Logic is a way of knowing nothing with confidence."

Naive idealism, further, is often translated into the form of a personal fable in which adolescents assume that their experience and thought are unique to their time and place in "history." A belief in the omnipotence of the individual is also reflected in adolescents' view that they are immune to the consequences of their actions, so that, for example, pregnancy as a result of sexual intercourse is "an event that happens to others." Similarly, many adolescents have an ideal view of parenthood and fail to take into account the complexities involved in raising a child. From the negative feedback perspective, the discrepancy between reality and the personalized ideal state of parenthood may contribute to the problems inherent in helping an adolescent become a good parent. Nevertheless, despite the caveats, adolescence signals the appearance of the ability to reason combinatorially, to evaluate verbal propositions without reference to concrete reality, and to chart hypothetical avenues of action. These abstract, analytical-reasoning skills bear implications for the social world of the adolescent.

SOCIAL DEVELOPMENT

The processes involved in the organization of interpersonal events have much in common with those involved in the organization of intrapersonal events (Feffer, 1970; Keating & Clark, 1980). The discussion here focuses on two avenues of interpersonal understanding—person perception and interpersonal relations—to elaborate the social implications of the advances in thought discussed above.

Person Perception

Person perception is a process of organization of information about persons in which consistent properties or traits are attributed to individuals. These traits, in turn, are integrated so that the behaviors and characteristics of others are viewed as having a dynamic causative impact on future behavior (Barenboim, 1981). For example, an adolescent might observe a classmate disrupt a teacher's lesson. Depending on other dimensions of the observer's organization, he or she might decide that the disruption implies such other concomitant traits as "disrespectful," "ignorant," "bored," and so on, or might attribute to the disrupter a different set of properties, such as "rebellious" or "intelligent but troubled." On the basis of repeated observations of behavior samples, the observer draws a sketch of the other person whereby the actor's behaviors are viewed as indicators of various components of an overall organization, often termed a "personality." From the viewpoint of self-regulation, greater complexity in the observer's perceptions of the other enables the observer to predict the other's future behavior. Prediction, in turn, makes it easier for the adolescent to engage in social roles with others, such as dating.

Conversely, failing to construct a person perception system of sufficient complexity may lead to frequent failures in interacting with peers and may contribute to depression (Rowe, 1978). Sally, for example, a 16-year-old adolescent who presented herself to a local mental health clinic as chronically depressed, tended to describe others solely in terms of a unidimensional good-bad continuum. Every trait seemed to imply every other trait; for instance, "meanness" implied "snotty"; but, it also implied other features that might not typically be associated with "meanness," such as "works a lot" and "dresses up well." From the perspective of a self-regulating system, Sally's comparative lack of differentiation in her interpersonal organization implied that she would experience difficulty in constructing standards and in matching her behavior to those standards. Thus, if a person were perceived by Sally as "mean," then Sally would also expect that person to exhibit a wide variety of other characteristics and behaviors. Sally's attempts to predict the behavior of others were, therefore, inevitably frustrated, since virtually any behavior at all could be equally anticipated within her implicit personality network.

A consistent lack of validation from others led Sally to the prediction that *any* action that she took was bound to result in a failure to successfully reduce the discrepancy between her perceptions and her standards, however globally and imprecisely the latter were defined. Failure in prediction, in turn, resulted in behaviors by Sally that included attempting to avoid contacts with peers and not bothering to get out of bed in the morning. Paradoxically, a consistent failure in prediction resulted in her certainty of failure—so why should Sally bother to get up in the morning?

Recall that a characteristic of successful plot enactment often involves the subordination of minor plots or features to major themes. Similarly, in order to anticipate the behavior of others successfully, Sally's system had to allow certain features, such as "meanness," to exclude other features, such as "dresses well." In addition, it was helpful from Sally's predictive framework if persons who were mean generally tended to be "snotty," "class clowns," and so on. Accordingly, the overall intervention goal with this adolescent involved an attempt to have her construct a more differentiated interpersonal world in order to more successfully anticipate a greater range of social inputs. Role-playing techniques (Kelly, 1955) were used to facilitate dialogue between the therapist and Sally. The therapist's efforts were aimed at offering a variety of alternative ways for Sally to think about persons and events in her life. The focus of intervention was on the development of interpersonal organization, not on "insight" or reinforcement schedules. Subsequent to intervention, Sally described herself as feeling less depressed and better able to sustain relations with peers. Concomitantly, her view of others was relatively more differentiated and hierarchically integrated (e.g., "anger" no longer necessarily implied "badness") and was, presumably, a more useful guide for her efforts to construe the behaviors of others.

Other Developments in Person Perception

With increasing age, adolescent descriptions of others tend to become more focused and hierarchically organized, with greater use of motivational and personal-orientation categories. Adolescents are therefore more likely to talk about the reasons or intentions underlying another person's behavior rather than focus on overt behaviors, as do younger children. In other words, adolescents construct a syntax for use in the prediction of behavior, whereas younger children have to remember separate behaviors. Since the memory of separate behaviors is relatively demanding, younger children may have greater difficulty in relating to new social events; adolescents can more readily extrapolate from their experience and so integrate interpersonal novelty. In addition, adolescents are willing to draw upon the conclusions of others in forming an impression of a target person; thus, there emerges in adolescence a concern for one's reputation—the perception of self by others (Livesley & Bromley, 1973; Wegner & Vallacher, 1977).

This more abstract mode of representation also has implications for an individual's self-conception. In early and middle childhood, self-conceptions are often based on concrete referents, such as body image, possessions, citizenship, and territoriality; in adolescence, on the other hand, the categories of self often comprise interpersonal style, ideology, occupational role, and self-determination (Montmayor & Eisen, 1977). In forming an impression, an adolescent is apparently more willing to suspend judgment and use first impressions tentatively, whereas a younger person operates immediately on the first set of information perceived. Presumably, these differences reflect the adolescent's transition from concrete to formal operations (Palmquirt, 1979). The greater differentiation and integration in adolescent impressions allows for an adaptation to a greater range of social events. But, greater complexity of thought may also create new conflicts, such as a perception of loneliness.

Adolescent Loneliness

The development of a network of trait implications, in conjunction with the emerging ability to reason in terms of possibilities, leads the adolescent to construe a distinction between real and apparent characteristics of both others and self (Selman, 1980; Wegner & Vallacher, 1977). Broughton (1981) has noted that adolescents often resolve the dialectic between existence and experience by adopting a dichotomy between a "real," inner self and an external/front self: the inner self tends to be equated with a *mind*, whereas the outer self is a fabrication—a *product of that mind*. Furthermore, the rationale for maintaining an inner sanctum is the belief that self-disclosure violates the sanctity or uniqueness of the individual. Thus, a certain degree of loneliness may be essential for the adolescent, since disclosure risks the loss of uniqueness and "a non-unique self is no self" (Broughton, 1981, p. 22).

Interpersonal Relations

The other avenue commonly explored in understanding interpersonal events emphasizes the importance of interpersonal relations as the source of social understanding. Mead (1934) has suggested that the mind is a conversation constructed in social interaction with others; categories of thought are products of social exchange (Damon, 1979). By positing existence as relational, the key question for any individual concerns not "What should I do?" but "What do you do when I do this?" (Youniss, 1980). Changes that occur in the individual's understanding of friendship during adolescence illustrate how cognitive development influences social exchange.

Friendship Selman (1980) and Selman and Selman (1979) have conducted a series of open-ended, semistructured interviews about a variety of interpersonal events. In each interview, an age-appropriate dilemma was presented, and subjects were asked to express their thoughts about the presented problem. In one dilemma, a teenage girl had to make a choice between keeping a date with a long-time friend or breaking it in order to accept an invitation from a new girl in town. Selman (1980) proposed that changes in one's understanding of social phenomena, such as friendship, are a manifestation of a developing ability to take the perspective of another. During early adolescence, perspective taking undergoes a transformation from the viewing of interpersonal relations as reciprocal, where each person is able to take the other's perspective, to the adopting of a generalized, third-person point of view. Thus, the above-mentioned ability to construct audiences implies that this audience, or a third-person perspective, can serve to monitor an interaction, thereby providing a larger context from which any dyadic interaction can be analyzed. That is to say, interpersonal relations can be taken as an object for further reflection.

Corresponding to the shift in perspective taking, the focus of early adolescent friendship shifts from a foundation of self-serving reciprocal cooperation (fair-weather friendship) to a broader conception of a friendship as an ongoing, mutual collaboration. Friends share more than agreements or plans; friends share feelings and help each other solve personal problems (Selman & Selman, 1979). Yet, close friendships in early adolescence may also contain provisions for the exclusion of others, violation of which may provoke jealousy on the part of the "injured" party.

During mid- to late adolescence, the individual comes to see friendship as something more complex, where both partners must be aware of the needs of each other but must also realize that they may not meet all those needs. The conception of friendship at this developmental juncture allows a friend to develop independent relationships: friendship is now seen as requiring both dependency and autonomy. Indeed, from the viewpoint of self-regulation, the evolution of a more elaborate cognitive structure in relation to the standard—friendship—implies a greater potential for constructing a "close" friendship, in that both partners adapt to new inputs to the system. The introduction of a third partner, for instance, is not necessarily destabilizing, even if one partner does not like the friend's friend.

Peer Relations   In addition to changing one's conceptions of friendship and the nature of interpersonal relations, the adolescent must integrate two, often competing, interpersonal worlds—those of parents and of peers. According to the Piaget-Sullivan thesis (Youniss, 1980), the two worlds of the adolescent reflect two distinct types of reciprocal relations. The first type, a relation of constraint or conformity, involves a socialization process, where child and adult interact with the emphasis on the adult's viewpoint; thus, the adult seeks to obtain compliance from the child.

In contrast, in the second type, a relation of cooperation, both persons are agents and recipients of instruction, and, potentially, the meanings each brings to the event are equally valid. Through the practice of relations of cooperation, the child's tendency toward subjective understanding is counteracted by the opposition of another's equally valid viewpoint. The primary socializing agent in the Piaget-Sullivan thesis is, therefore, the peer group. In adolescence, the discrepancy between relations of constraint and relations of cooperation becomes more apparent; the preferred way to reconcile the two relations is to engage in cooperative relations with both parents and peers. However, parents may not be prepared to change the basis of the relationship from one of constraint to one of cooperation.

Peer Conformity   The stereotypical view of adolescence suggests that an increase in peer interaction is accompanied by an increase in conformity to peers and a decrease in conformity to parents. Brendt (1979) has found, however, that conformity to peers peaks during mid-adolescence and then declines. During mid-adolescence, parental and peer beliefs often conflict. By the end of high school, parent and peer relations have generally entered another phase, one in which conflict between the two worlds is confined to a few issues. The curvilinear relation between age and conformity probably reflects the rise in mutual respect that is engendered by the development of interpersonal understanding during adolescence. As Samuel Clemens was once heard to comment, "when I was a boy of 14 my father was so ignorant I could hardly stand to have the old man around. But when I got to be 21, I was astonished at how much the old man had learned in seven years."

Implications of the Development of Interpersonal Understanding

Within the framework of the development of perspective taking during adolescence, the counselor-client relationship necessarily involves the coordination of the counselor's viewpoints with those of the adolescent parent. The goal of the interaction is dialectical exchange, not prescription. Thus, a counselor might encourage an adolescent to adopt the perspective of others involved in the relational network by asking, "How (and why) are your parents going to react?" "Your best friend?" The counselor could then reciprocate by expressing her or his reasoning about the meaning, responsibilities, and aftermath of pregnancy.

Another critical component in counseling teenage parents is teaching them about their children, in the sense that good parenting, at any age, involves an appreciation of the perspective of the developing child (Mancuso, 1979). Teaching adolescent parents about their children may be especially difficult if the stage of the parents' cognitive development precludes an ability to take their own thought as an object. It is difficult enough to be a parent, much less to think about alternative ways of parenting.

Adolescent parenting occurs in a multidimensional context. For purposes of clarity, the discussion here has focused on accomplishments of adolescent development within isolated domains. The final section of this chapter focuses on the integration of adolescent pregnancy and parenting in the sociocultural context of family and peers.

FAMILY SYSTEMS

A systemic approach helps focus on two elements identified in Chapter 1 as dominant themes in adolescent pregnancy: 1) the timing of pregnancy in the overall sequence of events that characterize an individual's life and 2) the interaction of the various sociocultural and individual components of development that lead to the pregnancy itself.

At the sociocultural level of analysis, pregnancy is a behavior that occurs within a homeostatic context of family and peers; it may be viewed by them as a discrepant event, to which they react in a manner so as to reestablish a previously existing organization (e.g., roles, relationships, etc.). As conceptualized by Haley (1980) and Minuchin (1974), the family system defines a unit of organization, or structure, that includes members, each of whom is constantly evolving and changing (e.g., psychological development), and this forces the family system, as a unit, to reorganize and stabilize its structure as transitions occur. The influences of the growth of individual members on the sociocultural levels of family systems result in what Haley has called stages in the development of family structure and organization. These stages parallel transitions in each family member's development and require reorganization of other family members around extraordinary events (e.g., marriage, birth, leaving home, death).

If the unit of analysis is the family system, of which the adolescent is a member, pregnancy becomes an event of input to the functioning of the family structure. The family system must reorganize itself to incorporate a new member, the infant, as well as to reflect new roles and relationships (teen-mother, woman, grandmother, etc.). The adolescent's ability to make the transition to a new role is, to some extent, determined by the maturity of other developmental components. In the case of precocious pubertal development, the reproductive capacity may be fully mature, while other aspects of physical development may not. More often, aspects of cognitive development may not be sufficiently complex to allow the adolescent to successfully integrate the multiplicity of roles necessary for parenting and adulthood.

The authors have concentrated on the destabilizing aspects of pregnancy; yet, others have pointed out perspectives that would frame pregnancy as a stabilizing rather than an imbalancing event (Haley, 1980; Minuchin, 1974). That is, pregnancy may serve to stabilize a family system that must achieve equilibrium at a time of transition—e.g., when the adolescent is to leave home. Within Haley's (1980) framework, for example, violation of parental rules serves two functions: on the one hand, it announces independence of thought and action; on the other hand, it focuses the parents' attention on discipline, sanctions, and the closer observation of their errant adolescent.

A case example serves to illustrate the relations and reorganizing function of pregnancy within the family context. A family of a mother and her two adolescent daughters, ages 13 and 15, was recently restructured to include a new stepfather. The 15-year-old daughter was sexually and physically mature but congenitally mentally retarded. Her mental functioning placed her within the trainable range, which allowed her to attend special classes at the local high school with other exceptional peers. The family approached the local mental health clinic for help in disciplining and communicating with her. As the mother and stepfather had recently married, the family was going through an adjustment of living arrangements, rules, and relationships. This older daughter, though cognitively less developed, was behaving socially in ways similar to her peers and seeking to conform to their standards and expectations. This included wearing makeup and spending more time with peers than with family members. Also, she was faced with the task of defining a new role in the family that would allow her to take a more adult, responsible, and autonomous position now that more of the mother's attention was being spent with her new husband.

Given the cognitively limited alternatives available, the search for a new role resulted in her becoming pregnant. During the family's third visit to the clinic, they announced her pregnancy, which had by then progressed several weeks. On the surface, the family appeared to be upset and unhappy with their pregnant daughter, although abortion was not considered an option, due to their fundamentalist religious orientation. Yet, on observing the family's interactions, a different set of relationships became apparent. The mother now defined the older daughter as a woman (however disobedient) who had a set of responsibilities and activities to perform in preparation for the coming child. The pregnancy served as an organizing device, not just for the daughter, but for the rest of the family as well. This crisis provided a stabilizing focal point around which all family members could begin to define their roles and created greater cohesion as the bulk of the family's time was spent discussing the pregnancy and its effect on other family members.

This case illustrates several important aspects of systems interaction. In particular, it shows how problems may arise when precocious pubertal development occurs without congruent cognitive integration. Although in the current example the mismatch between physiological and cognitive systems is striking, nonetheless, the case history demonstrates how pregnancy may be viewed as a method of reducing role ambiguity in an unstable, transitional context of family and peers. In this case, pregnancy gave a visible sign of adult reproductive capacity and simultaneously provided a new element around which the family could restabilize. In some cases, pregnancy can result in the adolescent's remaining at home and allowing grandparent and mother roles to develop. Conversely, the adolescent may leave home but put an infant in her place, so that parent roles shift to grandparent roles and the adolescent becomes "adult," or independent.

Pregnancy may also play a stabilizing role in the context of peers. This would occur primarily where childbearing, within or without marriage, is viewed as an expected sign of maturity and accepted by the subcultural norms. In this instance, the female who remains childless may, in fact, be different from her peers and outside of norm expectations. This is particularly true in those socioeconomic strata where early pregnancy is considered one of the (limited) alternatives available for the expression of adult roles; because remaining childless would violate these subcultural standards, the adolescent acts to readjust interactions within the sociocultural system by becoming pregnant.

CONCLUSION

To understand pregnancy in adolescence, it is necessary to understand the interface between biological phenomena and the corresponding psychological and sociocultural systems. Adolescence is a period of transition, a natural product of transition is ambiguity, and pregnancy may serve either to increase this ambiguity or stabilize and define behavior. Adult childbearing and parenting, in contrast, carries with it a definite set of roles and expectations, which, additionally, can have a positive impact on a more organized individual. A systems perspective is a useful tool for discussion of the various components of adolescent development that contribute to adolescent pregnancy and parenting. And, because a systems framework is useful in analyzing a complex phenomenon at several levels of organization and change, it provides a basis and context for family intervention.

REFERENCES

Aries, P. 1962. Centuries of Childhood: A Social History of Family Life. Vintage Books, New York.

Averill, J. R. 1980. A constructivist view of emotion. In: R. Plutchik and H. Kellerman (eds.), Emotion Theory, Research, and Experience, Vol. 1. Theories of Emotion. Academic Press, New York.

Barenboim, C. 1981. The development of person perception in childhood and adolescence: From behavioral comparisons to psychological constructs to psychological comparisons. Child Development 52:129–144.

Bradway, K. P., and Thompson, C. W. 1962. Intelligence at adulthood: A twenty-five-year follow up. General Educational Psychology 52:1–14.

Brendt, T. J. 1979. Developmental changes in conformity to peers and parents. Developmental Psychology 13:608–616.

Broughton, J. M. 1981. The divided self in adolescence. Human Development 27:13–32.

Bullough, V. L. 1981. Age at menarche: A misunderstanding. Science 213:365–366.

Carver, C. S. 1979. A cybernetic model of self-attention processes. Journal of Personality and Social Psychology 37:1251–1281.

Chi, M. T. 1978. Knowledge structures and memory developments. In: R. S. Siegler (ed.), Children's Thinking: What Develops? Lawrence Erlbaum Associates, Hillsdale, N.J.

Clausen, J. A. 1975. The social meaning of differential physical and sexual maturation. In: S. E. Dragastin and G. H. Elder (eds.), Adolescence in the Life Cycle: Psychology Change and Social Context, pp. 25–46. John Wiley & Sons, New York.

Damon, W. 1979. Why study social-cognitive development? Human Development 22:206–211.

Elkind, D. 1967. Egocentrism in adolescence. Child Development 38:1025–1034.

Elkind, D., and Bower, R. 1979. Imaginary audience behavior in children and adolescents. Developmental Psychology 15:38–44.

Erikson, E. H. 1968. Identity: Youth and Crisis. Norton, New York.

Feffer, M. 1970. Developmental analysis of interpersonal behavior. Psychological Review 197–214.

Flavell, J. H. 1963. The Developmental Psychology of Jean Piaget. VanNostrand Reinhold Co., New York.

Flavell, J. H. 1977. Cognitive Development. Prentice-Hall, Englewood Cliffs, N.J.

Frisch, R. E., and Revelli, R. 1970. Height and weight at menarche and a hypothesis on critical body weights and adolescent events. Science 169:397–399.

Green, R. S. 1969. Age-intelligence relationship between ages 16–64: A rising trend. Developmental Psychology 1:618–627.

Haley, J. 1980. Leaving Home: The Therapy of Disturbed Young People. McGraw-Hill Book Co., New York.

Hall, G. S. 1904. Adolescence: Its Psychology and Its Relations to Physiology, Anthropology, Sociology, Sex, Crime, Religion, and Education, Vol. I. Prentice-Hall, Englewood Cliffs, N.J.

Inhelder, B., and Piaget, J. 1958. The Growth of Logical Thinking from Childhood to Adolescence. Basic Books, New York.

Jones, M. C. 1965. Psychological correlates of somatic development. Child Development 36:899–911.

Kangas, J., and Bradway, K. P. 1971. Intelligence at middle age: A 38-year follow-up. Developmental Psychology 5:333–337.

Keating, D. P., and Clark, L. V. 1980. Development of physical and social reasoning in adolescence. Developmental Psychology 16:23–30.

Kelly, G. 1955. A Theory of Personality: The Psychology of Personal Constructs. Norton, New York.

Keniston, K. 1960. The Uncommitted: Alienated Youth in American Society. Dell, New York.

Lewis, C. C. 1981. How adolescents approach decisions: Changes over grades seven to twelve and policy implications. Child Development 52:538–544.

Livesley, W. J., and Bromley, D. B. 1973. Person Perception in Childhood and Adolescence. John Wiley & Sons, New York.

Maccoby, E. E. 1963. Woman's intellect. In: S. M. Farker and R. H. L. Wilson (eds.), Man and Civilization: The Potential of Woman. McGraw-Hill Book Co., New York.

Malmquest, C. P. 1978. Handbook of Adolescence. Jason Aronson, Inc., New York.

Mancuso, J. C. 1979. Reprimand: The construing of the rule violator's construct system. In: P. Stringer and D. Bannister (eds.), Constructs of Sociality and Individuality. Academic Press, New York.

Mancuso, J. C., and Sarbin, T. R. The self narrative and the enactment of roles. In: T. R. Sarbin and K. Schaibe (eds.), Studies in Social Identity. Praeger, New York, in press.

Mead, G. H. 1934. Mind, Self, and Society. University of Chicago Press, Chicago.

Minuchin, S. 1974. Families and Family Therapy. Harvard University Press, Cambridge, Mass.

Montmayor, R., and Eisen, M. 1977. The development of self conceptions from childhood to adolescence. Developmental Psychology 13:314–319.

Mussen, P. H., and Jones, M. C. 1957. Some conceptions, motivations, and interpersonal attitudes of late- and early-maturing boys. Child Development 28:242–256.

Neisser, U. 1967. Cognitive Psychology. Appleton-Century-Crofts, New York.

Nesselroade, J. R., and Baltes, P. B. 1974. Adolescent Personality Development and Historical Change, 1970–1972. Monographs of the Society for Research in Child Development, Vol. 39, no. 1 (Serial No. 154).

Palmquirt, W. J. 1979. Formal operational reasoning and the primary effect in impression formation. Developmental Psychology 15:185–189.

Peskin, H. 1967. Pubertal onset and ego functioning. Journal of Abnormal Psychology 72:1–15.

Peskin, H. 1973. Influence of the developmental schedule of puberty on learning and ego functioning. Journal of Youth and Adolescence 2:273–290.

Piaget, J. 1970. Structuralism. Basic Books, New York.

Powers, W. T. 1973. Behavior: The Control of Perception. Aldine Publishing Co., Chicago.

Rowe, D. 1978. The Experience of Depression. John Wiley & Sons, New York.

Sarbin, T. R. 1977. Contextualism: The world view for modern psychology. In: A. W. Landfield (ed.), Nebraska Symposium on Motivation: Personal Construct Psychology, pp. 1–41. University of Nebraska Press, Lincoln, Nebr.

Schaie, K. W., and Gribbin, K. 1975. Adult development of aging. Annual Review of Psychology 26:65–96.

Selman, R. 1980. The Growth of Interpersonal Understanding. Academic Press, New York.

Selman, R., and Selman, A. 1979. Children's ideas about friendship: A new theory. Psychology Today, October.

Tanner, J. M. 1962. Growth at Adolescence. 2nd Ed. Blackwell Scientific Publications, Oxford.

Waddington, C. H. 1957. The Strategy of the Genes: A Discussion of Some Aspects of Theoretical Biology. Allen and Unwin, London.

Wegner, D. and Vallacher, R. 1977. Implicit Personality Theory. Oxford University Press, New York.

Youniss, J. 1980. Parents and Peers in Social Development: A Sullivan-Piaget Perspective. University at Chicago Press, Chicago.

Zacharias, L., and Wurtman, R. J. 1969. Age at menarche. New England Journal of Medicine 280:868–875.

3

Maternal and Infant Deficits Related to Early Pregnancy and Parenthood

Charles Granger

IF THE ADOLESCENT MOTHER and her infant survive pregnancy, the psychological and social conditions in which they find themselves will be bleak and, without intervention, lifelong. This statement is not made lightly: the mortality rate of teenage mothers is higher than among all other age groups (except those over 40), at 46.7 per 100,000 live births (Stickle & Ma, 1975). And, for the infant born to the mother under 16, life chances are greatly reduced. It is estimated that more than one-fourth of these infants will be of low birth weight and premature (i.e., under 36 weeks of gestation). Recent data on low birth weight infants indicate that they suffer a higher incidence of neonatal-related complications, such as respiratory distress syndrome, hypoglycemia, jaundice, and other metabolic and neurological disorders. Of the 3,159,958 total births in the United States in 1974, 233,750 were of low birth weight (i.e., less than 5½ pounds, or 2,500 grams). More than 56,000 of these babies died in the first month of life, and another 60,000 are at risk for a lifetime disability (NINDB, 1967).

Chapter 4 discusses major longitudinal studies that have been initiated in England and the United States to discover why some infants in the low birth weight group fail to survive and, if they survive, why they are at greater risk of being handicapped. The present chapter is concerned with the life conditions experienced by adolescent mothers and their children. It should be kept in mind that some mothers and their infants manage very well. The factors involved in why this is so are the subject of the latter part of this book.

PHYSIOLOGICAL OUTCOMES: MOTHER AND CHILD

The negative outcomes of teenage births have been subject to investigation for more than 70 years (Tredgold, 1908; Wallace Wallin, 1917). Early research indicated that chances of bearing a premature or low birth weight infant were highest for the below-16-year-old group.

A great deal of research has been conducted to determine whether the pregnancy of the adolescent differs from that of the older woman. Before the early 1960s, research in this area typically involved small subject populations drawn from one or only a few hospitals. The external validity of such studies is questionable, to say the least. Aznar and Bennett (1961) summarized much of this research and, in so doing, noted prematurity as the principal negative outcome of adolescent pregnancy.

Bochner (1962) compared the pregnancy experiences of 272 females under the age of 17 with those of 658 females between the ages of 20 and 29. Adolescent pregnancies were similar to pregnancies of the older women with three notable exceptions: the adolescent group showed higher incidences of toxemia, pelvic contraction, and prolonged labor. These conditions were particularly evident for the youngest adolescents (12- to 13-year-olds).

Israel and Wouteraz (1963) conducted one of the earliest studies on this subject, which carefully controlled for selection bias and used a large subject population. Ten hospitals were involved in the study, each of which served patients from a variety of racial groups and socioeconomic levels. Of 40,709 deliveries, 3,995 were to adolescents. When their pregnancy histories were compared with those of older women, significantly higher incidences of prematurity, toxemia, labor over 20 hours, one-day fever, and puerperal morbidity were noted for the adolescents.

In a retrospective study conducted by Coates (1970), the pregnancy experiences of 137 primigravidas (women pregnant for the first time) under the age of 14 were compared with those of a matched group of 2,968 older primigravidas. Despite nonsignificant differences in prenatal care, young adolescents exhibited significantly higher incidences of toxemia, mild and severe preeclampsia, and/or eclampsia. A higher but nonsignificant incidence of anemia was also found.

Perhaps the single, most problematic outcome of the adolescent's pregnancy is the tendency for it to end prematurely and produce a low birth weight infant. Grant and Heald (1972) reviewed 40 years of literature on the complications of adolescent pregnancy and found that "every study from that of

Posner and Pulver in 1935 through that of Semmens in 1968 has shown that adolescents have a statistically significant, higher rate of prematurity (birth less than 2500 grams) than a comparison group of older mothers'' (p. 569).

More recent research has lent further support to those findings. Nortman (1974), reporting data obtained from the U.S. Vital Statistics Division, has stated that significantly more infants weighing less than 2,500 grams are born to both very young mothers and mothers in their 30s. Stickle and Ma (1975) have reported similar findings, indicating that national birth statistics for 1973 show that nearly 16% of mothers under the age of 15 years delivered infants weighing less than 2,500 grams. This can be compared with a rate of less than 7% for mothers between the ages of 20 and 29. Even more alarming is the incidence of infants who weigh less than 2,000 grams. For mothers younger than 15, the incidence of this is nearly 7%, while for mothers in their 20s, the incidence is about 2%.

Hogue (1978) reviewed pregnancy and birth histories for all live births (1968-1973) to women under the age of 24 who were living in four counties in North Carolina. Hogue's study population was relatively homogeneous (i.e., poor, white) and contained a high incidence of adolescent childbearing. Results of that study indicated twice the incidence of low birth weight to mothers younger than 17 than to older mothers.

Premature and low birth weight infants characteristically have a difficult time adjusting to extrauterine life and demonstrate this difficulty through a number of subsequent developmental problems. Caputo and Mandell (1970) have reviewed much of the literature in this area and identified a number of specific negative developmental sequelae. These include intellectual impairment (for very low birth weight infants), hyperkinesis, autism, involvement in early childhood accidents, language delays, academic achievement problems, growth impairment, motor impairment, and neurological dysfunction. Although causes vary, minimal brain dysfunction is presumed to mediate many of these delays. Even though recent improvements in newborn care have slightly diminished these impairments (Davies & Stewart, 1975), negative outcomes persist.

Infants of young mothers experience health problems in addition to low birth weight. Menken (1972) has demonstrated, for instance, that neonatal and postnatal mortality rates are higher for infants of adolescent mothers than for infants of mothers in their 20s. Neonatal mortality rates are twice as high for infants born to women younger than 15 than for those born to women of age 20 to 30. Similar data are reported by Nortman (1974). Also, Broman (1980) has found that Apgar scores at 1 and 5 minutes after birth for infants of young mothers were lower than for infants of older mothers. Prematurity and low birth weight, however, remain the predominant health hazards for infants of adolescent mothers.

SOCIAL OUTCOMES

Mothers

After the negative physical outcomes that are evident during and shortly after pregnancy, a host of negative social outcomes await many adolescent mothers and their infants. It can be said that life opportunities are significantly diminished for the adolescent mother. Apparently, this process begins with the disruption of her schooling.

The Educational Research Services' Office of Adolescent Pregnancy Programs (1980; Pregnant teenagers, 1970) has found that one-third of 154 school systems surveyed (with 12,000 or more students) required young mothers to leave regular educational settings as soon as their pregnancies were discovered. This policy has since been prohibited by the regulations of Title IX of the Education Amendments of 1972. According to those regulations, pregnant girls and young mothers are entitled to complete their educations with full access to resources and facilities provided by the public school system; further, their attendance in specially designed programs is voluntary. According to the above-cited survey, however, such attendance is infrequent. Of 17,000 school systems surveyed, only one-third provided special educational services for pregnant adolescents.

Furstenburg (1976) has reported similarly discouraging statistics. In that study, fully one-half of adolescent mothers had failed to graduate from high school by 5 years after childbirth. Apparently, this was not due to a lack of interest in completing their schooling, since one-half of those who did not graduate had attempted to return to school after childbirth, and 16% of this group were still enrolled in school.

Hardy, Welcher, Stanley, and Dallas (1978) have reported even more disturbing data. Only 35% of adolescent mothers in their study had completed high school by the time their children were 12 years old. This figure is less than half that of a comparison group of older mothers (77%). Similar results were found by Russ-Eft, Sprenger, and Beever (1979), who indicated that pregnancy and marriage were listed as the most frequently reported reasons for dropping out of school.

In addition to education disruption, adolescent pregnancy disrupts marriage and family relationships. In Furstenburg's (1976) study, marriage histories of adolescent mothers in Baltimore were compared with those of women who became pregnant and married in their 20s. An interview conducted 5 years after each subject's delivery indicated clear differences between subject groups. While only 3% of adolescent mothers had been married at the time of their child's conception, this figure increased dramatically to 20% at the time of the first prenatal visit and to 25% by the time of delivery. This increase suggests the (catalytic) influence pregnancy had on the timing of marriage plans. Further evidence of this is provided by examination of the comparison group, where only 21% were married by age 18, compared with 41% of adolescent mothers. Indeed, the adolescent mothers seem to have been aware of the influence their pregnancies had on their marriage plans: only one in three felt that the timing of her marriage was consistent with her wishes for the future.

Not surprisingly, adolescent marriages are characterized by high dissolution rates. In the aforementioned study, 20% of adolescent marriages ended in separation within 1 year. Percentages increased to 45% by 3 years and to 60% by 6 years. Classmates of these adolescents who did not become pregnant during early adolescence experienced marriage dissolution rates of about one-half of these figures.

Hardy et al. (1978) have reported similar data. Over a 12-year period beginning with the birth of a first child, only 18.8% of adolescent mothers experienced no change in marital status. Of young mothers studied, 26% underwent one change, 17% underwent two changes, and 37%, three or more changes. This is strikingly different from the experiences of older mothers, of whom nearly 40% underwent no change in marital status, and 32%, one change. Adolescent pregnancy, then, appears to contribute significantly to marital instability.

Adolescent mothers, whether by preference or not, are less likely to work than are mothers who first give birth in their 20s. Data cited in the Alan Guttmacher Institute (1976) report indicate that 19 months after delivery, fully 91% of adolescent mothers had neither full- nor part-time employment. Seventy-two percent of these women were receiving welfare benefits, a proportion approximately 4.6 times that among women who first gave birth in their 20s.

Furstenburg (1976) has characterized husbands of adolescent marriages as inexperienced and unskilled applicants in the labor market: "Most of these men have low earning potential before they ever wed. An ill-timed marriage may further limit their prospects by compelling them to terminate school and enter the labor force under less than favorable circumstances" (p. 156).

Hardy et al. (1978) have reported that 36% of adolescent mothers reported incomes below $5,000 per year, nearly twice the proportion for older mothers in the comparison group. At 7 years after childbirth, only 44% of adolescent mothers were independent of public assistance. This figure remained unchanged at the 12-year follow-up (5 years later). In contrast, 66% of older mothers were free of public assistance at the 7-year follow-up, that figure increasing slightly to 71% at the 12-year follow-up.

Similar data have been reported by Clapp and Raab (1978). In their study, 60% of adolescent mothers reported that Aid to Families with Dependent Children (AFDC) was their sole source of income. Interestingly, although only 40% reported being employed, 77% had been employed at some time after the birth of a first child. Apparently, maintaining employment after having a child was difficult.

Research also indicates that women who marry and/or have their first child very early in life tend to have additional children more rapidly than do older mothers. Keeve, Schlesinger, Wight, and Adams (1969) studied birth certificates of infants born to mothers between the ages of 12 and 19 in a middle-Atlantic metropolitan county between 1958 and 1967. Their successive births indicate the tendency of such mothers to have large, closely spaced families.

Hardy et al. (1978) have found a marked difference between adolescents and older mothers in the number of children born during a 12-year period following the mother's first child. During that period, adolescent mothers had an average of 3.25 children, significantly more than the 2.35 average for older mothers. And, since adolescent mothers were farther away from the end of their childbearing period than were older mothers, this difference could be expected to increase.

The Broman (1980) summary of the Collaborative Perinatal Project has indicated that the adolescent mother of the lower social class tends to be unmarried, be on welfare, have a lower educational attainment, and, in general, be downwardly socially mobile. These findings are similar to R. Smith's (1980) report of rural teenage pregnancies. In addition, Smith's study sheds light on the personality characteristics of these adolescent mothers. They tend to have persistent problems in interpersonal relationships, little self-insight, and low self-esteem. They tend to feel that events control them (external locus of control) and that what has happened to them was beyond their own control. They lack close friends and confidants. As one of Smith's (1980) case studies reported, their feeling is that, "Well, all of my life, nothing goes right" (p. 53). Tolstoy said that the world's worst prison is poverty; it may be added that the mother and child who live in this "world prison" are among the most disadvantaged.

A study conducted in Canada has revealed marked differences between the adolescent mother who keeps her baby and the one who places her child for adoption (Lightman & Schlesinger, 1980). The keepers are more likely both to have suffered serious psychological illness and to be unmarried or, if married, become divorced. The nonkeepers tend to finish school and to be less likely to seek support from a social agency.

As more middle-class adolescents become pregnant and bear children, evidence of psychopathology among pregnant teenagers is decreasing (P. B. Smith, 1982). Psychopathology rates are highest among the lowest social class; because of this, imputations of a cause-effect relationship between adolescent pregnancy and psychopathology are unwarranted.

Middle-class teenagers who become pregnant tend to have greater support systems (P. B. Smith, 1982; R. Smith, 1980) with which to face general social rejection and the burden of the responsibilities of raising a child. For lower-class pregnant teenagers, on the other hand, adoption may well be the "one" solution, as Lightman and Schlesinger (1980) suggest.

Parent-Child Interactions

Clearly, to say there is one parenting style for adolescents and one for adults would be nonsense. As reported in other chapters, there can be marked social class differences in childrearing. The parenting practices found largely in the lower class, but not exclusively so, are the ones that have been shown to be nonfacilitating for the children's development (Sameroff, 1979; Werner, Bierman, & French, 1971).

From the available research, it is not easy to identify the childrearing practices that are typical of adolescent parents. The few studies on adolescent parenting that do exist have revealed interesting findings, however. Sears, Maccoby, and Levin (1957) were, perhaps, the first to describe the parenting styles of young mothers. Unfortunately, in their sample, young mothers were also predominantly less educated and had lower incomes than did the older mothers used for comparison purposes. Effects of age alone, then, were difficult to specify. Nonetheless, observations of young mothers with their children were revealing. The widely held societal belief at that time, according to Sears et al. (1957), was that young mothers were "more relaxed, more spontaneously warm, and more able to cope with the demands of child care" (p. 436). Contrary to this perception, their study observed young mothers as "more irritable, in that they were quick to punish, more likely to quarrel with their husbands, and somewhat more likely to express an underlying feeling of hostility toward their children" (p. 437). The authors speculated that the need to settle down to childrearing and the inability to participate in activities common to their age group led to a sense of frustration which may have been directed at the perceived cause of their life situation, namely, their children. These findings are supported by other studies reported by Phipps-Yonas (1980), which suggest that adolescent mothers are less emotionally involved with their infants, offer less stimulation through talking, and provide less intellectual encouragement.

In a study of adolescent couples, de Lissovoy's (1973) findings are remarkably similar. In his research, 48 couples residing in semirural areas in central Pennsylvania were studied. Again, many couples were not high school graduates, and many had low incomes. De Lissovoy's discouraging summary follows:

> In general, I found the young parents in this study to be, with a few notable exceptions, an intolerant group—impatient, insensitive, irritable, and prone to use physical punishment with their children. Only five mothers, for example, expressed enjoyment of their children in the sense that they spontaneously cuddled or played with them just for the sheer joy of it. It was also surprising to learn

that in this primarily rural area only three mothers had attempted to breastfeed their children (pp. 22–23).

Responses obtained from questionnaire items on developmental milestones were consistent with these observations. When asked to estimate when their infants would first be able to sit alone, walk, talk, recognize a wrongdoing, be toilet trained, and so on, adolescent couples uniformly erred in the direction of overestimating the speed of development, sometimes by several months.

Parents were also asked about the amount of crying they should expect from a baby who is fed and dry. One-third of the mothers and two-thirds of the fathers expected little or no crying and advocated little tolerance of crying in such situations.

Regarding physical punishment, de Lissovoy noted that spanking and slapping an infant's wrist, hand, or face were common practices once infants were able to crawl. To the question, "How often do you spank?" typical answers were, "When he deserves it," "It depends on what he has done," and "When I can't take it any longer." Virtually all mothers responded in a manner indicating the use of spanking as punishment, and all but two mothers indicated that their husbands also spanked the child.

Other research in this area has yielded strikingly different results. Osofsky and Osofsky's (1970) research involved the observation of adolescent mother-infant dyads before and during pediatric visits. Adolescent mothers typically demonstrated a great deal of warmth toward their infants but engaged in little verbal interaction. Infants, on the other hand, were active but relatively unresponsive toward their mothers. These conflicting observations suggest that there are other factors, such as low socioeconomic status (SES) and social background, associated with parenting styles that make it difficult to generalize within the adolescent group.

Another study (Epstein, 1979), involving 98 pregnant adolescents and their subsequent children, drew its subject population from parent education programs and adolescent health clinics located in southeast Michigan. While these results may have questionable application to pregnant adolescents in general (many of whom do not or cannot avail themselves of such services), they are, nonetheless, of interest here.

Pregnant adolescents were given a card-sort task and viewed videotapes in order to determine their knowledge of child development and facilitative caretaking practices. The general finding, according to Epstein, was that pregnant teenagers expected too little too late from infants. In other words, adolescents typically underestimated both needs and abilities of their infants at various developmental levels.

This was not the case for every area of development. Items that tapped knowledge of basic care, health and nutrition, and perceptual and motor development were answered relatively accurately. In contrast, items regarding cognitive, social, and language development found adolescents attributing needs and abilities to infants many months too late. Unfortunately, this uneven knowledge profile may merely reflect emphases of programs attended by the subjects.

Subsequent observations of adolescent mothers with their infants have yielded results similar to those described by Osofsky and Osofsky (1970). That is, adolescent mothers were observed to frequently display affection for their infants. But, as in the earlier study, they seldom spoke with their infants or engaged in playful interactions, which are so conducive to development.

Results of research done by Granger (1981) are very similar to these. In that study, a multiple-choice test regarding the time of emergence of developmental milestones was given to 371 13- and 14-year-olds. The subject population was dissimilar to that of previous research efforts in that both males (173) and females (198) were tested, all of whom had had no formal instruction in child care or child development, and none of whom had ever been parents.

Similar to Epstein's (1979) findings, adolescents' expectations regarding development were typically inaccurate. Estimations of when infant abilities develop yielded mean error scores of 5 to 7 months. Adolescents' expectations were significantly less accurate for cognitive and social abilities than for motor and language abilities, and their expectations were significantly less accurate for abilities that develop in the first year of life than for those that develop in the second year. Furthermore, adolescents exhibited late expectations about twice as often as they did early expectations. More specifically, they overestimated more often than not the actual time of emergence of various infant abilities.

Sex differences found were as expected. Females uniformly displayed more accurate expectations regarding development than did males. The females could by no means be characterized as a knowledgeable group, however, since the size of their errors was nearly as large as that of their male contemporaries.

Field, Widmayer, Stringer, and Ignatoff (1980) administered questionnaires to adolescent and older mothers that were designed to tap their knowledge of child development and parenting attitudes. When infants were 4 months old, adolescent mothers indicated both less realistic expectations and less optimal attitudes than did the older mothers.

As this review indicates, research in each of the areas of adolescents' knowledge of child development and adolescent parenting styles is far from conclusive. While de Lissovoy (1973), for instance, found that adolescents overestimate the speed of development, Epstein (1979) concluded that they hold accurate expectations in certain developmental areas (i.e., basic care, health and nutrition, and perceptual and motor development) and underestimate the speed of development in others (i.e., cognitive, social, and language development).

Findings related to adolescent parenting styles are equally puzzling. While Sears et al. (1957) and de Lissovoy (1973) found adolescent parents to be irritable, impatient, and intolerant, Osofsky and Osofsky (1970), Epstein (1979), and Field et al. (1980) found them warm and loving but neither verbally nor intellectually stimulating, as was also reported by Phipps-Yonas (1980).

Reasons for these conflicting findings are uncertain. It should be noted that subject populations have been both urban and rural and have differed in the number and kinds of pregnancy-related services to which they have been exposed. Also, test instruments designed to assess knowledge of child development have, with the exception of Epstein's (1979), contained very few items. Their validity and reliability, then, are open to question.

It is perhaps unreasonable to assume that adolescent parents, or parents of any age group, comprise a homogeneous population. Ethnic, economic, religious, and a host of other demographic variables could account for large differences in knowledge of child development and parenting styles.

SUMMARY

From this review, it is clear that both the adolescent mother and her child may be destined for an array of negative physical and psychosocial outcomes. For infants of adolescent mothers, the principal health problems are those associated with premature birth and low birth weight. Research conducted from as early as the turn of the century has shown higher incidences of these two health problems, while recent research has indicated that they have an impact upon the course of subsequent development. Related subsequent delays and disabilities include intellectual impairment, hyperkinesis, language delays, academic achievement problems, motor impairment, neurological impairment, and others.

The adolescent mother herself experiences, first of all, a more difficult pregnancy than do women in their 20s. While a number of pregnancy complications have been identified, those most commonly found have been toxemia and anemia. The mortality rate among young mothers reflects the severity of teenage obstetric complications.

One must keep in mind that most of the research on outcomes of adolescent pregnancy have dealt with low SES populations and contained large samples of black and Spanish-surname mothers. Recent data with older adolescents (17- to 19-year-olds) have indicated that the outcome of these pregnancies are not always unfavorable, particularly in middle-class groups. In addition, when the adolescent mother has a support system in the form of a family or husband, the life chances of the mother and child are greatly enhanced (LaBarre, 1972; Wise & Grossman, 1980).

As the adolescent mother begins her career as a parent, psychosocial problems predominate. Educational attainment is decreased, income levels are lower, and reliance on public assistance is higher. Marital instability is increased, with higher rates of divorce and separation. Also, persistent emotional and interpersonal difficulties are common. Compounding these problems, adolescent mothers tend to have more children more rapidly than do women who have their first child when in their 20s.

Research has also indicated that the adolescent mother is ill-equipped to provide a caregiving environment that facilitates her child's development. Some research in this area has found adolescent mothers impatient with and intolerant of their children, and virtually every study has found them to hold unrealistic expectations regarding child development. The only encouraging finding comes from those observations of adolescent mothers treating their children in an affectionate manner. Unfortunately, these same mothers were observed to be intellectually nonstimulating. The parenting ability of adolescents is, therefore, of particular concern.

The list of maternal and infant deficits associated with early pregnancy and parenthood reviewed here should provoke concern—but not despair. It is important to bear in mind that these outcomes typify the course of events in the absence of intervention. Appropriate intervention, of a multifaceted nature, could likely alleviate many of these problems.

REFERENCES

Alan Guttmacher Institute. 1976. 11 Million Teenagers: What Can Be Done About the Epidemic of Pregnancies in the United States. New York.

Aznar, R., and Bennett, A. E. 1961. Pregnancy in adolescent girls. American Journal of Obstetrics and Gynecology 81:934.

Bochner, K. 1962. Pregnancies in juveniles. American Journal of Obstetrics and Gynecology 83(2):269-271.

Broman, S. H. 1980. Outcome of adolescent pregnancy: A report from the Collaborative Perinatal Project. In: S. Harel (ed.), The At Risk Infant, pp. 45-49. Excerpta Medica, Amsterdam.

Caputo, D. V., and Mandell, W. 1970. Consequences of low birthweight. Developmental Psychology 3(3):363-383.

Clapp, D. V., and Raab, R. S. 1978. Follow-up of unmarried adolescent mothers. Social Work (March)149-153.

Coates, J. B. 1970. Obstetrics in the very young adolescent. American Journal of Obstetrics and Gynecology 108(1):68-72.

Davies, P. A., and Stewart, A. L. 1975. Low birthweight infants: Neurological sequelae and later intelligence. British Medical Bulletin 1:85-90.

de Lissovoy, V. 1973. Child care by adolescent parents. Children Today (July-August)22-25.

Educational Research Services. 1980. Office of Adolescent Pregnancy Programs Information Bulletin. Vol. 1, no. 1.

Epstein, A. S. 1979. Pregnant teenagers' knowledge of infant development. Paper presented at the Biennial Meeting of the Society for Research in Child Development, March, San Francisco.

Field, T. M., Widmayer, S. M., Stringer, S., and Ignatoff, E. 1980. Teenage, lower-class, black mothers and their preterm infants: An intervention and developmental follow-up. Child Development 51(2):426–436.

Furstenburg, F. F. 1976. The social consequences of teenage parenthood. Family Planning Perspectives 8(4):148–164.

Granger, C. R. 1981. Young adolescents' knowledge of child development. Unpublished doctoral dissertation, Indiana University, Bloomington.

Grant, J. A., and Heald, F. P. 1972. Complications of adolescent pregnancy. Clinical Pediatrics (October)567–570.

Hardy, J. B., Welcher, D. W., Stanley, J., and Dallas, J. R. 1978. Long-range outcome of adolescent pregnancy. Clinical Obstetrics and Gynecology 21(4):1215–1231.

Hogue, C. J. R. 1978. Are teenagers really at higher risk? Paper presented at the 106th Annual Meeting of the American Public Health Association, October, Los Angeles.

Israel, S. L., and Wouteraz, T. B. 1963. Teenage obstetrics. American Journal of Obstetrics and Gynecology 85:659.

Keeve, J. P., Schlesinger, E., Wight, B., and Adams, R. 1969. Fertility experience of juvenile girls: A community-wide ten-year study. American Journal of Public Health 59:2185.

LaBarre, M. 1972. Emotional crises of schoolage girls during pregnancy and early motherhood. Journal of the American Academy of Child Psychiatry 11(2):537–555.

Lightman, E. S., and Schlesinger, B. 1980. Nonmarried mothers in maternity homes. Paper presented at the 57th Annual Meeting, American Orthopsychiatric Association, April 9, Toronto, Canada.

Menken, J. 1972. The health and social consequences of teenage childbearing. Family Planning Perspectives 4:54–63.

National Institute of Neurological Diseases and Blindness (NINDB) Research Profile. 1967. Summary of Research Reported by the U.S. Department of Health, Education, and Welfare, Washington, D.C.

Nortman, D. 1974. Parental age as a factor in pregnancy outcome and child development. Reports on Population/Family Planning. Population Council, New York.

Osofsky, H. J., and Osofsky, J. D. 1970. Adolescents as mothers: Results of a program for low-income pregnant teenagers with some emphasis upon infants' development. American Journal of Orthopsychiatry 40(5):825–834.

Phipps-Yonas, S. 1980. Teenage pregnancy and motherhood: A review of the literature. American Journal of Orthopsychiatry 50(3):403–431.

Pregnant teenagers. 1970. Today's Education 59:9.

Russ-Eft, D., Sprenger, M., and Beever, A. 1979. Antecedents of adolescent parenthood and consequences at age 30. The Family Coordinator (April)173–178.

Sameroff, A. J. 1979. The etiology of cognitive competence: A systems perspective. In: R. B. Kearsley and I. E. Sigel (eds.), Infant at Risk: Assessment of Cognitive Functioning, pp. 115–152. Erlbaum Associates, Hillsdale, N.J.

Sears, R. R., Maccoby, E. E., and Levin, H. 1957. Patterns of Childrearing. Row and Peterson, Evanston, Ill.

Smith, P. B. 1982. Reproductive health care for teens. In: M. Sugar (ed.), Adolescent Parenthood. Spectrum Pub. Inc., Jamaica, N.Y.

Smith, R. 1980. High risk families in rural communities, characteristics of pregnant teenagers and their families: A report from the Kauai study and community follow-up. In: S. Harel (ed.), The At Risk Infant, pp. 50–61. Excerpta Medica, Amsterdam.

Stickle, G., and Ma, P. 1975. Pregnancy in adolescents: Scope of the problem. Contemporary Ob/Gyn (June).

Tredgold, A. F. 1908. Mental Deficiency. William Wood and Company, New York.

Wallace Wallin, J. E. 1917. Problems of Subnormality. World Book Company, New York.

Werner, E. E., Bierman, M. J., and French, F. E. 1971. The Children of Kauai. University Press of Hawaii, Honolulu.

Wise, S., and Grossman, F. K. 1980. Adolescent mothers and their infants: Psychological factors in early attachment and interaction. American Journal of Orthopsychiatry 50(3):454–468.

4

The Longitudinal Studies

Nicholas J. Anastasiow

There is a general agreement in child development that family environments constitute a powerful influence on the development of the young child.
—Nihira, Meyers, and Mink, 1980

AS EARLY AS 1843, physicians noted that some infants born at risk for retardation and handicapping conditions survived infancy and were perceived to be normal as adults, whereas others who survived infancy were severely retarded and incapacitated as adults (Neligan, Prudham, & Steiner, 1974).

Why some infants who suffered breech birth or anoxia at birth were able to survive and to function in the normal intellectual range was a puzzle that motivated several longitudinal studies across the world. At last count, there were more than 20 such studies, but the discussion here is limited to three major efforts that have not only measured and monitored physical growth and maturation but have also assessed psychological and social variables. As seen below, it is in the psychosocial domain that the critical variables that predict the infant's later, normal or abnormal functioning in the elementary school have been detected.

In the discussion that follows, one should keep in mind that infants who suffer perinatal stress have a higher death rate than do other infants. Thus, the factors discussed that appear related to overcoming perinatal stress have been taken from the survivors of the first months of life following stress. Major advances have been made in the survival chances for low birth weight and premature infants. More and more severely damaged infants are living, due to the success of high-risk nurseries. In spite of the efforts of the caregiver, however, these severely damaged infants may never attain normality. This chapter focuses on the environmental events that enhance the chances of the moderately to mildly damaged infant for achieving normality. In addition, it deals with how low birth weight and premature infants who are predicted to be at risk for retardation can be assisted in order to reverse such a probability.

THE LONGITUDINAL STUDIES

A comprehensive study in Newcastle-upon-Tyne in England has attempted to investigate Lilienfeld and Pasamanick's notion of a "continuum of reproductive casualty" (Neligan et al., 1974, p. 2). The investigators wished to detect where in the continuum one might expect to find serious damage versus moderate or mild damage and what the physiological correlates of damage were.

To do so, they followed a 3-year birth sample (1960–1962) by collecting the obstetric and perinatal data on 14,000 survivors of the first month of life and following them to school age.

The major findings of their study show that even two of the most lethal perinatal factors—breech birth and anoxia—produce only trivial effects in terms of brain damage. The most potent factors were grouped as biological and social ones.

The important biological factors were sex and birth weight. Boys were at greater risk than girls, as were the lower birth weight infants. The authors concluded that low birth weight produced effects consistent with the notion of a continuum of reproductive casualty. That is, low birth weight is associated with higher infant death, brain damage, and mental retardation.

Social factors, the second group, had a greater impact on development than did biological ones. Social class and the quality of the mother's care of her child in the home had a stronger association with the abnormal functioning of the stressed child than did any other variable or set of variables.

In later sections of this chapter, the quality of the mother's care is defined more specifically than was done by the Newcastle-upon-Tyne group. In their study, quality of care was assessed by nurses visiting the home, who used subjective criteria. Nevertheless, in spite of the subjectiveness of the nurses' reports, what a mother (usually the major caregiver) does in the home with her child drastically influences the child's developmental outcome.

THE COLLABORATIVE STUDY

Broman, Nichols, and Kennedy's collaborative (1975) study was designed to investigate beliefs about the effects of pre- and perinatal trauma on childhood intelligence (p. vii). The investigators researched the relationships of 169 prenatal and postnatal variables for 26,760 children born to mothers in 12 collaborating research centers throughout the United States.

Their 1975 report presents the relationships of these 169 variables and the 4-year-old IQ of children in the sample. Of the 169 variables, 73 were significantly correlated with IQ in the white population and 59 in the black population, with an overlap of 49 in both populations (p. 289). The highest correlates with IQ for whites were maternal education, social class, and non-verbal intelligence. For blacks, the highest correlations were with motor test scores at 8 months, mental test scores at 8 months, social class, and maternal education.

Thus, in a group of 169 other factors, social class and maternal factors appear among the highest predictors of a child's IQ. The variance of IQ is explained more by social class and maternal variables than by the presence of perinatal complications. These findings are consistent with what was found in the Kauai study, which is discussed below.

THE KAUAI STUDY

The Kauai study followed the outcome of over 3,000 pregnancies on the island of Kauai and examined the outcome of the live-born children and their families into the child's adolescent period. The 2-year and 10-year status of these children are reported in *The Children of Kauai* (Werner, Bierman, & French, 1971). Their adolescent status is discussed in *Kauai's Children Come of Age* (Werner & Smith, 1977) and in *Vulnerable But Invincible* (Werner & Smith, 1981).

The Kauai study is unique in that its multidisciplinary team was composed of pediatricians, psychologists, and public health workers. In addition, it measured a set of psychosocial invariables, such as maternal education and years of schooling, rather than global-cluster scores. Further, the study observed *all* the children in a whole community and, as early as in the fourth week, observed social interaction in the home environment. The study has an added uniqueness in that the composition of the sample included United States citizens of Filipino, Japanese, Chinese, Korean, Hawaiian, Portuguese, and Caucasian descent.

Werner et al.'s findings support and extend the results of the two studies reported above: "In general, the more severe the perinatal complications and the more unfavorable the home environment, the more retarded was the physical and intellectual development of the child by age two" (p. 54).

Such variables as parental language styles, stimulation, concern for and emotional involvement with the child, and parental attitudes toward achievement make a major impact on the child's intellectual status before 2 years of age.

The authors of the Kauai study have suggested that it is necessary to provide enriched environments before the age of 2. They conclude their

4-year data analysis with the statement that "children suffering from moderate to severe perinatal stress need to be identified early and efforts made to provide them with a supportive and stimulating environment to minimize the effects of perinatal damage" (p. 60). The authors further conclude that the damaging effects of poor environments have an impact on normal infants, as well, and that compensation efforts should begin by or before age 2.

The 10-year follow-up study confirmed these earlier results as well as the impact of educational stimulation received in the home. A difference of as much as 20 IQ points was noted between children from high- and low-educational-stimulation homes. Educational stimulation was defined as the providing of a good verbal model, extending the child's vocabulary, and making books available. The accompanying facilitative childrearing practices were low use of physical punishment and the use of warmth.

Emotional and educational support appeared to facilitate recovery from perinatal stress. In the absence of these two factors, children who suffered perinatal stress contributed overwhelmingly to Kauai's school failures and mentally retarded and emotionally disturbed population. In addition, children who were normal at birth but resided in homes of low stimulation and low emotional support also became members of the abnormal school population.

A summary statement of the Kauai group warrants repeating, particularly since the volume is out of print.

> The Cattell IQs at two years for group 1 (no perinatal stress and favorable home environment) ranged from 137 (superior) to 88 (low average); no child in this group had a score of more than one standard deviation below the mean.
> The range of Cattell IQs of Cattell IQs for children in group 2 (severe perinatal stress, but favorable postnatal environment) was from average to low average (105–86); one child with severe anoxia did not participate in the first follow-up, but was tested when entering school and received a Stanford-Binet IQ of 138.
> Children in group 3 (no perinatal stress, but unfavorable home environment) had Cattell IQs ranging from 112 to 74. More than one-half of these children scored below IQ 90, in the "slow learner" range. The range of Cattell IQs in group 4 (severe perinatal stress and unfavorable home environment) was from 89 to 20. All children in this group had "below average" Cattell IQs and four of the children had already been identified as mentally retarded.
> A similar contrast between these groups emerges from the findings of the independent pediatric examinations. The children in group 1 without perinatal stress who lived in a favorable environment were rated, with only one ("low normal") exception, either superior or normal in physical status. Pediatric examinations showed few handicaps and health problems among the children who survived severe perinatal stress and grew up in a favorable postnatal environment (group 2). Only one child in this group, prematurely born, was considered "physically retarded" at the time of the two-year follow-up.
> Of the children without perinatal stress who had grown up in an unfavorable home environment (group 3), nearly one-third had ratings of "low normal" physical status, lowered vitality, and malaise, malnourishment, and evidence of physical neglect. With one exception (a 46-week postmature infant), all of the children who had been exposed to both severe perinatal stress and an unfavorable

home environment (group 4) were rated "below normal" in physical status. In this group, one child was diagnosed as a cretin, and one had a diagnosis of microcephaly and spastic quadriplegia by age two.

The two groups of children who grew up in an early environment rated favorable (groups 1 and 3) were more often described as "determined," "persevering," "sociable," "friendly," "independent," "active," "energetic," "responsive," characteristics that are more extroverted and adjusted. This was true both for the children with and without perinatal stress.

In contrast, the two groups of children who had grown up in a family environment rated unfavorable (groups 2 and 4) were more often described as "bashful," "shy," "slow," "fearful," "dependent," "solemn," "uncommunicative." These introverted, maladjusted characteristics occurred more often among children who had also undergone severe perinatal stress.

The 10-year-old data are equally impressive:

The case summaries also illustrate characteristic changes in developmental status from two to 10 years for the four groups of children, representing the favorable and the unfavorable ratings on the "environmental quality" and "perinatal stress" dimensions.

Group 1, the children without perinatal stress who grew up in homes rated favorable in environmental stimulation and emotional support, had 10-year IQs in the superior (128) to average (101) range. No child had achievement problems in school, and all except one had gained IQ points since the two-year follow-up—an average gain of 13 points, with a range from 2 to 28 points.

Group 2, the children who had suffered severe perinatal stress but grew up in homes rated favorable in educational stimulation and emotional support, had 10-year IQs ranging from 125 to 96, from the superior to the average range. One-fourth of these children had some achievement problems, but the overwhelming majority functioned adequately in school. One-sixth had significant physical problems. All children on whom Cattell test scores were available had gained an average of 13 IQ points, an increase similar to the group without perinatal stress which was exposed to a favorable environment.

Group 3, the children without perinatal complications who grew up in homes rated unfavorable in educational stimulation and emotional support, had 10-year IQs ranging from 123 to 70. More than half of these children had IQs below 85, in the "slow learner" or "educable mentally retarded" range. Intelligence quotient point changes from two to 10 years were erratic, ranging from +37 to −20, with an average loss of four IQ points. With one exception, all of the children in this group had serious achievement problems in school; four-fifths also had behavior problems. Nearly two-thirds of the children had verbal subtest scores significantly lower than performance test scores, indicating a serious language disability. Only two children had significant physical defects.

Group 4, the children who suffered severe perinatal stress and also grew up in homes rated unfavorable, had a very wide range of IQs at age 10, from 117 to 30. One-half of the children in this group were either "slow learners" or mentally retarded; four-fifths had serious achievement problems; one-fourth had serious behavior problems; and one-fourth had perceptual problems. All but three of the children who had Cattell test scores reported a loss in IQ points since the two-year follow-up. One-third had significant physical defects of the central nervous and the musculoskeletal systems.

The Kauai authors have also reported that other longitudinal studies have found that children of unconcerned parents have lower IQs than do demanding parents who encourage their children to develop. The next section demonstrates that the basic caregiver's knowledge of facilitative childrearing practices may be the key to the fulfillment of a child's genetic potential, regardless of stress.

FUNCTIONAL PARENTAL INTELLIGENCE

Early studies of the effects of orphanages on children's intellectual development provided the intellectual base for both the Kauai study and those studies reported below. Although these studies of orphanages were attacked severely in their time, they have survived the burden of those early criticisms and provided the field with provocative data. Skeels (1966) has found that infants raised by institutionalized mentally retarded women did much better on cognitive measures than did infants left under the care of a nurse with 14 other infants.

Skeels and Dye (1939) followed a group of adopted children to their adult status and found the adopted group fared well on a host of educational and social measures, whereas the unadopted group had lower occupational status and in some cases were still institutionalized with below-70 IQs. The stimulation of the environment was suspected as the contributing factor of the adopted children's success.

In a series of important studies, Hunt (1976, 1979) varied the adult-pupil ratio in various Greek orphanages. He found that a 1:1 ratio resulted in the normal functioning of the child, whereas a high 15:1 ratio resulted in infant deaths, retardation, and other abnormal results.

Carrying his work further, in orphanages in Iran, Hunt, Mohandessi, Ghodssi, and Akiyama (1976) varied the adult-child ratio and the nature of the educational stimulation to the infants. The results at age 6 clearly demonstrated that low nurse-child ratios and having nurses (caregivers) who provide language stimulation and warmth encourage (or push) children toward achieving developmental milestones and lead to children who achieve and/or accelerate beyond developmental norms.

For Hunt, caregiving stimulation is central in assisting children to reach their potentials, which Hunt believes can be attained by all but a minute portion of the world's children. Hunt (1980) notes that "the more similar the childrearing conditions of individuals are, the smaller is the variance among individuals of attaining developmental landmarks and in measures of development in educational achievement" (p. 15). For example, children of Oriental Jews of professional status and of working status who settled in Kibbutzim have very similar IQs, whereas those working classes who settled in cities have IQs 30 to 40 points below those of the professional class.

Clearly, childrearing conditions, rather than genes, account for the differences.

Hunt's general findings have been supported by the Milwaukee Project: Garber and Heber (1976) found that among the very poorest among the black inner-city population in Milwaukee, mother's intelligence was highly correlated with infant's intelligence. They hypothesized that if genetic cause determined this relationship, environmental stimulation would not affect children born to 75- to 80-IQ mothers who lived in deep poverty.

To test out their notions, the authors identified 40 women whose IQs were 75 and lower who resided in the lowest socioeconomic area of Milwaukee. The area had the highest number of condemned housing units, the highest welfare rate, and the lowest employment rate. The mothers and their offspring were randomly divided into two groups. One group, the control, received no attention. The second group was provided with intensive day-care and preschool program stimulation at low caregiver-child ratios, beginning before the child was 1 year old and continuing until the child entered the first grade. The mothers in the experimental groups received some rehabilitation employment training. The results are remarkable. The experimental group of children *all* had IQs in the normal range at age 10. The control group did not fare so well. Control group children tended to have IQs of 80 and below; many were below 70. What is identified by these investigators and by the studies of facilitating caregivers in Kauai, England, Greece, and Iran is referred to as "functional maternal intelligence."

A set of practices commonly held by most middle-class parents across the world includes the provision of verbal models and stimulation, low use of physical punishment, moderate use of warmth and emotional support, and a push to achieve.

Caldwell and colleagues Elardo and Bradley have systematically investigated the home environment of lower socioeconomic families in a series of studies (Bradley & Caldwell, 1978; Elardo, Bradley, & Caldwell, 1975, 1977). They have found that the nature of the home environment is the best predictor of the child's IQ and language development. Mothers who support their children, provide stimulation, and encourage development have children who attain the normal ranges of IQ and language development. Mothers who do not, have children with below normal IQs and achievement problems. That a large number of lower-class parents, both black and white and of various ethnic groups, fail to provide these facilitating practices is the concern of this book.

SUMMARY

Longitudinal studies have revealed that it is the nature of the caregiving environment, particularly in the infancy period before 2 years of age, that influences the child's IQ and verbal development. What is known suggests that the global factors of emotional support, push toward development, verbal and educational stimulation, and low physical punishment blend to facilitate a child's development even in cases of low birth weight, prematurity, anoxia, and breech birth.

The negative impact of high physical punishment, neglect, lack of stimulation, and lack of encouragement is so strong as to depress IQs and achievement in the normal child and to have profound effects on the stressed child.

The growing number of adolescent parents who are unaware of facilitating practices is of grave concern when one considers that low birth weight and prematurity have greater incidences among very young mothers.

But much can be done. Chapter 5 speculates as to why the first 2 years of life seem to be so critical for IQ and language development; in addition, results from infant and other intervention programs are examined. Chapter 6 presents programs designed to teach the adolescent, and Chapter 7 discusses the results of such programs.

REFERENCES

Bradley, R. N., and Caldwell, B. M. 1978. Screening the environment. American Journal of Orthopsychiatry 48(1):114–130.

Broman, S. H., Nichols, P. L., and Kennedy, W. A. 1975. Preschool IQ. Erlbaum Associates, Hillsdale, N.J.

Elardo, R., Bradley, R., and Caldwell, B. N. 1975. The relation of infants' home environments to mental tests performance from six to thirty-six months: A longitudinal analysis. Child Development 46:71–76.

Elardo, R., Bradley, R., and Caldwell, B. N. 1977. A longitudinal study of the relation of infants' home environment to language development at age three. Child Development 48:595–603.

Garber, H., and Heber, H. 1976. The Milwaukee Project: Indications of the effectiveness of early intervention to prevent mental retardation. In: P. Mittler (ed.), Research to Practice in Mental Retardation, Vol. 1: Care and Intervention. University Park Press, Baltimore.

Hunt, J. M. 1976. Environmental programming to foster competence and prevent mental retardation in infancy. In: R. N. Walsh and W. T. Greenough (eds.), Environments as Therapy for Brain Dysfunction, Vol. 17: Advances in Behavioral Biology. Plenum Publishing Corp., New York.

Hunt, J. M. 1979. Psychological development: Early experience. In: M. R. Rosenzweig and L. W. Porter (eds.), Annual Review of Psychology. Vol. 30, pp. 103–143. Annual Reviews, Inc., Palo Alto, Calif.

Hunt, J. M. 1980. Implications of plasticity and hierarchical achievements for the assessment of development and risk of mental retardation. In: D. B. Sawin, R. C. Hawkins, L. O. Walker, and J. H. Penticuff (eds.), Exceptional Infant, Vol. 4, pp. 7–54. Brunner/Mazel, New York.

Hunt, J. M., Mohandessi, K., Ghodssi, M., and Akiyama, M. 1976. The Psychological Development of Orphanage-Reared Infants: Interventions with Outcomes (Tehran). Genetic Psychology Monographs, Vol. 94, pp. 177–226.

Neligan, G., Prudham, D., and Steiner, H. 1974. Formative Years: Birth, Family, and Development in Newcastle-upon-Tyne. Oxford University Press, London.

Nihira, K., Meyers, C. E., and Mink, I. T. 1980. Home environment, family adjustment, and the development of mentally retarded children. Applied Research in Mental Retardation 1:5–24.

Skeels, H. M. 1966. Adult Status of Children with Contrasting Early Life Experience. Monographs of the Society for Research in Child Development, Vol. 31, no. 3, pp. 1–65.

Skeels, H. M., and Dye, H. B. 1939. A study of the effects of different stimulation of mentally retarded children. Proceeding of the American Association on Mental Deficiency 44:114–136.

Werner, E. E., Bierman, J. M., and French, F. E. 1971. The Children of Kauai. University Press of Hawaii, Honolulu.

Werner, E. E., and Smith, R. S. 1977. Kauai's Children Come of Age. University Press of Hawaii, Honolulu.

Werner, E. E., and Smith, R. S. 1981. Vulnerable But Invincible: A Longitudinal Study of Resilient Children and Youth. McGraw-Hill Book Co., New York.

5

The High-Risk Infant and the Socioeconomically At-Risk Child

Nicholas J. Anastasiow

IF THE EFFECTS of the environment on intellectual and language development are so strong during the infancy period, are they as powerful in offsetting a lack of stimulation in later years? Further, what is the rationale to account for the powerful effects of the environment and the caregiver on intellectual and language development during the first 2 years of life? Can the effects of a lack of stimulation and/or neglect be overcome later in the child's life? These questions form the central core of this chapter, which first treats the hypotheses of the brain's plasticity and then examines the effects of a variety of programs designed to provide stimulation for infants born at risk for retardation or other handicapping conditions.

BRAIN PLASTICITY

In recent months, arguments against the positive effects of early stimulation have captured the interest of the medical profession (Ferry, 1981). Not intending to do so, medical professionals have alarmed parents as to whether or not early treatment and stimulation will harm or assist their handicapped children.

The title of Ferry's (1981) article, *On Growing New Neurons: Are Early Intervention Programs Effective?* distorts the issue. No serious professional ever claimed that stimulation would grow new neurons, but it has been noted that a facilitating environment can make serious alterations in the dire predictions of some disorders, such as anoxia (Sameroff, 1979) and low birth weight (Werner & Smith, 1977).

It has been well established, for example, that malnutrition during early infancy has an impact on the infant's later cognitive functioning. Further, severely malnourished infants appear to have cognitive damage even when put on a nourishing treatment program. Richardson (1976), however, has found that the long-term effects of the malnourishment do not appear as cognitive deficits in some children. In cases where deficits do not occur, one finds the child has been reared in a supportive and facilitative environment.

Sameroff (1979) has emphasized the positive impact that the caregiver and an enriched environment can have on anoxia victims. Among children who survive, those who have experienced a supportive and enriched environment score at age 6 in the normal range of intelligence scores. The contrast group, which has experienced a negative environment, score as many as 30 points lower. These results are similar to those reported in Chapter 4. Data from animal research present some interesting implications as to what the role of an enriched environment may be for humans.

Vernadakis (1982) and Greenough (1975) have stated, essentially, that the brain is sensitive to experience during the time that the immature sections of the brain are undergoing maturation of structure. For lower animals, such as the rat, most of the brain is mature at birth, and the immature structures complete maturation shortly after birth. In spite of the very limited time in which environmental enrichment can have an impact on the development of these structures, the data currently available suggest that dramatic environmental effects can be identified in both the rat and higher-order mammals, where the brain is less mature at birth. The present discussion does not intend to simplify the subject, for the data on brain development can fill volumes in itself. However, the point to be made is, specifically, that experience assists the brain to complete development and in some cases facilitates maximal development.

Greenough (1978) has summarized a series of studies examining the impact of an enriched environment on animals' developing brains. He reports that the impact of experience results in more dendrites and synaptic junctions between neurons in the area of the brain affected. Neurons communicate with other neurons through dendrites, which receive activity from other neurons across the synapses. Therefore, finding more dendrites and synaptic junction suggests that experience results in a more mature communication facility of the neurons. Further, animals raised in an enriched environment, one in which they can act on that environment, learn mazes more rapidly, have thicker cerebellar cortexes, have larger cortical neuronal cell bodies, more glial cells, and more synaptic connections between cells (Rosenzweig, Bennett, & Diamond, 1972).

Greenough, in a series of studies, has found that training has a lesser effect on the brain than does enriched experience, and that the young brain is more susceptible to impact than are older brains. Older brains can be influenced, however, and training does have some impact on their structure. In addition, it is not only the more newly evolved sections of the brain that have been affected by enriched environments; effects have been demonstrated as well on the hippocampus and paraflocculus of the cerebellum (Floeter & Greenough, 1979).

Rosenzweig and his colleagues have shown that rats that have been brain damaged and then raised in an enriched environment tend to show fewer effects of ablation and less spread of lesion than do rats that have been damaged and raised in a deprived environment.

The general consensus (Chall & Mirsky, 1978) is that, at birth, the brain has the capacity and potential for establishing innumerable pathways and connections. Early activity and stimulation enhances the development of synaptic connection among neurons.

From an evolutionary perspective, the active experiencing of a social environment is critical to the fulfillment of what has been coded in the genes (Jerison, 1973). Motivation to learn and the capacity to learn are, in all probability, genetically transmitted capabilities (Fishbein, 1976), and, therefore, environmental enrichment and learning through caregivers would seem to be as important and as necessary a part of evolution as hair color. For man, the brain's central role is to create a model of the world that enables the nervous system to handle vast amounts of information received through the senses (Jerison, 1973); the brain acts as a reducing mechanism (Bergson, 1926). But, sensory systems mature only after birth: vision reaches nearly full maturation during the first years of life, and hearing, during the fifth decade of life (Lecours, 1975). Thus, although both the nervous and sensory systems are activated by genetically fixed behavior patterns, they are dependent upon environmental information for maintenance. Kittens and chimpanzees raised in the dark fail to see when placed in the light (Chall & Mirsky, 1978). Blind children present the social smile at age 3 months, triggered genetically as a fixed behavior pattern (formerly called instinct); however, being unable to see smiles in return, they soon stop smiling.

In man, fixed behavior patterns initiate actions that are dependent on environmental events for full maturation. These fixed behavior patterns are associated with sensory systems, which are designed to be flexible and to allow for learning in the environment. Thus, biological intelligence is the capacity to construct perceptual worlds and, because of the flexibility of this perceptual system, to allow for great diversity in the construction of images, languages, and cultures. For the same reason that the biological advantage of immaturity at birth enables or invites structures to mature in a variety of environments, if the environment does not provide the experiences that activate, maintain, and stimulate the development of these perceptual systems, serious delays in development can occur. Thus enriched environments not only facilitate development and assist in moderating or reducing the effects of stress but are necessary and essential for basic human development. Just as enriched environments make a substantial difference in the brain development of animals, so, too, the environment and the nature of the caregiver's childrearing practices make a substantial difference in humans as well (as demonstrated in the longitudinal studies reported in Chapter 4). Evidence to further support these inferences has been gained from intervention studies.

PRESCHOOL INTERVENTIONS

Most of the early intervention studies have been conducted with children who live in poverty and, thus, are not pure, experimentally designed studies of the impact of the environment; rather, they study the effects of environmental enrichment on children who are poor.

Poverty includes a host of variables. Poor populations show higher reproductive risk, more low birth weight babies, higher incidence of maternal infections, greater lack of prenatal care, greater malnutrition or undernutrition, higher ratio of anemia, more frequent illness, less use of health care facilities, larger family size, less maternal attention, and less stimulation (Farran, Haskins, & Gallagher, 1980; Schoggen & Schoggen, 1981). Intervention with poor children is therefore seen by many as a total, ecological approach rather than as the mere removal of the child from the home for several hours of schooling per day.

As has been demonstrated in the studies by Garber and Heber (1981) and Hunt (1961, 1976, 1979), intervention in the total environment of the child from birth through 5 years of age leads to normal cognitive functioning at age 6. The issue regarding the effects of later intervention with children who have been raised in less stimulating environments or who have suffered a sensory impairment of some nature is still not completely resolved, but early results are very encouraging. Those from the Head Start social experiment and other intervention programs with children of lower socioeconomic settings are impressive (Lazar, Hubbell, Murray, Rosche, & Royce, 1977; Zigler & Valentin, 1979). The major impact of such programs has been medical—in terms of improved health: children who have experienced Head Start are generally healthier; many childhood disorders have been corrected, while others have been avoided.

Schweinhart and Weikart (1980) followed a group of randomly assigned Head Start children and their controls up to their 16th birthdays. They found that many positive social gains had been made that could be linked to the early Head Start experience. There were fewer Head Start students in special education classes, and fewer had been retained in grade. The Head Start children were seen by their parents and teachers as being more academically and vocationally oriented. They were rated higher on personal social skills, and more were employed in part-time, after-school jobs.

Schweinhart and Weikart (1980) have noted in their study, and in an analysis of the combined results of eight other early intervention studies, that the major impact of early childhood intervention has been a resultant decrease both in the number of children placed in classes for the mentally retarded and in the number retained in grade. When one considers that the cost of special education is double that of regular education, these findings bear great societal significance. Because mental retardation and/or grade retention are closely associated with lower educational attainment and, in consequence, lower occupational status, the chief impact of early childhood programs may be in providing its participants with the higher educational attainment and resultant higher income to help some of them break out of the poverty cycle.

EARLY INTERVENTION WITH HANDICAPPED CHILDREN

Early treatment and stimulation can markedly improve the social and cognitive functioning of children exhibiting a wide variety of sensory impairments and disorders (Tjossem, 1976). Studies have documented a higher level of functioning in children in early childhood programs for those with physical disabilities, visual impairments, Down's syndrome, and language disorders, among others (see particularly pp. 335–668, Tjossem, 1976). Intervention rarely cures the child, but it can markedly improve the child's life chances and functioning.

Dramatic results have been demonstrated with children who are hearing impaired (Horton, 1974) and blind (Fraiberg, 1977). Horton has noted that intervention with hearing-impaired children before age 3 can result in their being placed in the regular classroom and treated as "normal." And, thereafter, they will be able to develop normal speech and language. Speech in the early-treated hearing-impaired child may not be as precise in terms of pronunciation as in the child who hears normally, but neither is it as hollow and distorted as that in hearing-impaired persons treated later in life. In addition, the early-treated hearing-impaired child's language tends to be correct in word order and meaning, whereas the later-treated child may have some difficulty with word order and abstract meanings. Thus, the failure to intervene early results in greater economic costs, for treating and providing treatment for the older child, as well as in great human loss, that of relegating these individuals to isolation from mainstream society because of their inability to communicate orally.

Fraiberg (1977) has noted that blind children who are not provided extrasensory stimulation during the first year of life to offset their lack of vision may develop mutism and autistic-like behaviors. Blind children who experience intervention can function as normal.

It is very difficult to determine whether mental retardation is also present in deaf and blind children. The rubella epidemic of the 1960s created a large population of deaf-blind children, some of whom were mentally retarded and some not. Differentiating the retarded and nonretarded children required early treatment to provide cognitive stimulation in the absence of the two sensory modes. By these efforts, some cognitively normal children were saved from a life of complete isolation (Appell, 1977); Sullivan's work with Helen Keller is a dramatic case in point (Lash, 1980).

As Ziarnik (1981) has noted, it is the improvement in social behaviors that does much to facilitate the handicapped child's movement out of the institution and into mainstream society. Early intervention can do much to eliminate features often considered negative, such as grimaces associated with the deaf. Northcott (1981) has reported that hearing-impaired children who receive early intervention do not develop these negative mannerisms.

Denhoff (1981) has reported a range of positive findings with high-risk, low birth weight infants. In one study, a 3-year enrichment program resulted in favorable outcomes for 90% of the participants; the benefits of early intervention included positive gains for parents as well as children. Denhoff has suggested, in fact, that the early intervention laid the groundwork for the emergence of positive developmental patterns. In his study, *no* motor delay was present in most of the infants with cerebral palsy.

Ohrt and Flehmig (1980) have found that treatment of motor impairment at 3 months of age resulted in normal motor development, whereas treatment at 6 months failed to improve the condition.

Schoggen and Schoggen (1981) have reported that positive results have been obtained with low birth weight babies by lowering the noise level in isolettes, taping the mother's voice into the isolette, and providing frequent visits and regular handling by the mother. These techniques resulted in weight and developmental gains for low birth weight infants.

DELAYED ADOLESCENCE

In impressive work done in Israel, Feuerstein (1980) has demonstrated cognitive gains through an "Instrumental Enrichment" program. The program stresses mediated learning, which interprets for students the meaning of their environmental encounters. In essence, Feuerstein claims that children who reside in poverty have not been adequately trained to observe and interpret the meanings of events they experience. Thus, these children fail to make acute discriminations and often do not note subtle differences. In turn, failure to note similarities and differences interferes with the ability to generalize.

Feuerstein's program constructs educational experiences in which the adult interprets the meaning to the student. Feuerstein feels that these students are deprived of their culture through lack of training by their parents. By calling attention to both the objective and subjective perceptual experience, these students can acquire the techniques to control and guide their own learnings. In reports of the program in Israel (Feuerstein, 1980) and in Nashville, Tennessee (Haywood & Wachs, 1981), impressive gains have been noted in the treated adolescents' achievement patterns.

SUMMARY

Intervention in the early years of a child's life can markedly improve the child's life chances and adult status. Intervention later in life can have marked effect, but rarely will a cure of the negative insult at birth be negated later in life (Clarke & Clarke, 1977). The evidence suggests that early identification, diagnosis, and treatment are the most desirable methods for the remediation of handicapping conditions. Further, the entire ecology of the child should be taken into account. Treating a child without assisting the family may have limited impact. Head Start, which provided nutritional, medical, and educational programs, had a valuable impact even though the child did not begin the program until age 4 or 5. The most impressive results have been those that affect the family and the child. In the case reported by Garber and Heber (1981), intervention made the difference whether the child lived life as a normal or as a retarded individual.

Evidence from animal research has clearly indicated that an enriched environment has a major impact on the developing young brain. Animals who are reared in an enriched environment, in which they are free to explore and which contains responsive objects, such as a ball, have heavier brains and areas of the brain in which there is more mature synaptic development with richer dendritic tree formation.

The greater impact of the enriched environment is on areas of the brain that have not fully matured (Vernadakis, 1982); consequently, to have an impact on brain development, the enriching experiences must come while the brain is still undergoing maturation. For the rat, whose brain is mostly mature at birth, that period occurs for a very short time just after birth. For humans, major areas of the brain are not mature at birth and are therefore capable of influence by environmental events during early periods of life.

Although Werner and Smith (1981) and Sameroff (1979) have not so specified, it can be assumed that the underlying biological reason why environments can influence recovery of trauma or insult at birth is that when the brain is not fully mature, it can be influenced by experience. Rosenzweig et al.'s (1972) research on brain-damaged rats supports this notion. They found that spreading of the brain-damaged area is reduced and recovery enhanced in damaged animals that are placed in enriched environments.

What, then, is the relationship of experience to maturation rates among groups of animals and humans? As has been noted, rats, whose brains mature rapidly, have only a short period in which the environment can influence certain areas of brain development. For humans, the period from birth to 18 months of age encompasses the major brain development, signaled by behavioral integrations at 2 to 3 months, 7 to 9 months, and 18 to 22 months. It is assumed that the behavioral integrations are accompanied by, caused by, or related to brain maturation.

What differential impact of experience can be speculated between a group of rapid developers and one of slower developers? It would seem that the more rapid developers would have a shorter period during which environmental enrichment could affect the brain than would the slower developers. Conversely, the greater the environmental deficit (lack of stimulation), the more negative its impact on brain development and its behavioral correlates.

In considering racial differences with regard to physical development, blacks tend to have a more rapid physical acceleration than whites. Thus, it can be argued that environmental deficits would have an even greater impact on blacks, due to the shorter period during which the related areas of the brain are maturing and thus responsive to environmental influence. Rates of development may play a critical role in achieving what is genetically possible. This is an unexamined area of research that should prove promising.

To be sure, the data are not final at present. Cure is not the major issue. What is critical is the improvement of the life status of handicapped children and their parents. In Denhoff's (1981) study, approximately 7% of the moderately involved physically disabled children were classified as normal after treatment, and the others improved in their ability to physically function more independently and perform some self-care rather than be completely dependent on others. It may be inferred that the independence of functioning greatly improved their quality of life.

REFERENCES

Appell, M. W. 1977. Infant stimulation programming for the deaf-blind. In: E. Lowell (ed.), The State of the Art: Prospectives on Serving Deaf-Blind Children. U.S. Department of Health, Education, and Welfare, Washington, D.C.

Bergson, H. L. 1926. Mind-Energy: Lecture and Essays. Henry Holt and Company, New York.

Chall, J. S., and Mirsky, A. F. 1978. Education and the Brain. University of Chicago Press, Chicago.

Clarke, A. D. B., and Clarke, A. M. 1977. Prospects for prevention and amelioration of mental retardation. American Journal of Mental Deficiency 81(6):523-533.

Denhoff, E. 1981. Current status of infant stimulation or enrichment programs for children with developmental disabilities. Pediatrics 67(1):32-37.

Farran, D. C., Haskins, R., and Gallagher, J. J. 1980. Poverty and mental retardation: A search for explanations. In: J. J. Gallagher (ed.), Ecology of Exceptional Children, pp. 47-65. New Directions for Exceptional Children, No. 1. Jossey-Bass, San Francisco.

Ferry, P. C. 1981. On growing new neurons: Are early intervention programs effective? Pediatrics 67(1):38-41.

Feuerstein, R. 1980. Instrumental Enrichment: An Intervention Program for Cognitive Modifiability. University Park Press, Baltimore.

Fishbein, H. D. 1976. Evolution, Development, and Children's Learning. Goodyear Publishing Co., Calif.

Floeter, M. K., and Greenough, W. T. 1979. Cerebellar plasticity: Modification of Purkinje cell structure by differential rearing in monkeys. Science 206(12):227-229.

Fraiberg, S. 1977. Insights from the Blind. Basic Books, New York.

Garber, H., and Heber, R. 1981. The efficacy of early intervention with family rehabilitation. In: M. Begab, H. Garber, and H. C. Haywood (eds.), Psychosocial Influences in Retarded Performance, Vol. II: Strategies for Improving Competence, pp. 71-87. University Park Press, Baltimore.

Greenough, W. T. 1975. Experimental modifications of the developing brain. American Scientist 63:37-46 (January/February).

Greenough, W. T. 1978. Development and memory: The synaptic connection. In: T. Teyler (ed.), Brain and Learning. Greylock Publishers, Stamford, Conn.

Haywood, H. C., and Wachs, T. D. 1981. Intelligence, cognition, and individual differences. In: M. J. Begab, H. C. Haywood, and H. L. Garber (eds.), Psychosocial Influences in Retarded Performance, Vol. I: Issues and Theories in Development, pp. 95-126. University Park Press, Baltimore.

Horton, K. B. 1974. Infant intervention and language learning. In: R. L. Schiefelbusch and L. L. Lloyd (eds.), Language Perspectives—Acquisition, Retardation, and Intervention. University Park Press, Baltimore.

Hunt, J. 1961. Experience and Intelligence. The Ronald Press, New York.

Hunt, J. 1976. Environmental programming to foster competence and prevent mental retardation in infancy. In: R. N. Walsh and W. T. Greenough (eds.), Environments as Therapy for Brain Dysfunction, Vol. 17: Advances in Behavioral Biology. Plenum Publishing Corp., New York.

Hunt, J. M. 1979. Psychological development: Early experience. In: M. R. Rosenzweig and L. W. Porter (eds.), Annual Review of Psychology, pp. 103-143, Vol. 30. Annual Reviews, Inc., Palo Alto, Calif.

Jerison, H. J. 1973. Evolution of the Brain and Intelligence. Academic Press, New York.

Lash, J. 1980. Helen and Teacher. Delacorte, New York.

Lazar, I., Hubbell, V. R., Murray, H., Rosche, M., and Royce, J. 1977. The Persistence of Preschool Effects. DHEW Publications (OHDS) No. 78-30129, U.S. Department of Health, Education, and Welfare, Washington, D.C.

Lecours, A. R. 1975. Myelogenetic correlates of the development of speech and language. In: E. H. Lenneberg and E. Lenneberg (eds.), Foundations of Language Development: A Multidisciplinary Approach, Vol. 1, pp. 121-135. Academic Press, New York.

Northcott, W. N. 1981. Freedom through speech: Every child's right. The Volta Review 83(3):162-181.

Ohrt, B., and Flehmig, I. 1980. The neurological evaluation of the newborn. In: S. Harel (ed.), The At Risk Infant, pp. 133–137. Excerpta Medica, Amsterdam.

Richardson, S. A. 1976. The influence of severe malnutrition in infancy on the intelligence of children at school age: An ecological perspective. In: R. N. Walsh and W. T. Greenough (eds.), Environments as Therapy for Brain Dysfunction, Vol. 17: Advances in Behavioral Biology. Plenum Press, New York.

Rosenzweig, M. R., Bennett, E. L., and Diamond, M. C. 1972. Brain changes in response to experience. Scientific American 226:22–30.

Sameroff, A. J. 1979. The etiology of cognitive competence: A systems perspective. In: R. B. Kearsley and I. E. Siegel (eds.), Infants at Risk: Assessment of Cognitive Functioning, pp. 115–151. Erlbaum Associates, Hillsdale, N.J.

Schoggen, P., and Schoggen, M. 1981. Ecological factors in the prevention of mental retardation. In: M. J. Begab, H. C. Haywood, and H. L. Garber (eds.), Psychosocial Influences in Retarded Performance, Vol. I: Issues and Theories in Development, pp. 47–64. University Park Press, Baltimore.

Schweinhart, L., and Weikart, D. 1980. Effects of Early Childhood Intervention on Teenage Youths. High Scope Monographs. High Scope Foundation, Ypsilanti, Mich.

Tjossem, T. D. (ed.). 1976. Intervention Strategies for High Risk Infants and Young Children. University Park Press, Baltimore.

Vernadakis, A. 1982. Epigenetic factors in neuronal differentiation: A review of recent research: In: R. N. Emde and R. J. Harmon (eds.), Attachment and Affiliative Systems: Neurobiological and Psychobiological Aspects. Plenum Press, New York.

Werner, E. E., and Smith, R. S. 1977. Kauai's Children Come of Age. University Press of Hawaii, Honolulu.

Werner, E. E., and Smith, R. S. 1981. Vulnerable But Invincible: A Longitudinal Study of Resilient Children and Youth. McGraw-Hill Book Co., New York.

Ziarnik, J. P. 1981. Preparing mentally retarded adolescents for successful societal adaptation: New curriculum challenges for public education. In: N. J. Anastasiow (ed.), Socioemotional Development, pp. 81–95. New Directions for Exceptional Children, No. 5. Jossey-Bass, San Francisco.

Zigler, E., and Valentin, J. (eds.). 1979. Project Head Start: A Legacy of the War on Poverty. The Free Press, New York.

6

Programs Designed To Respond to Adolescent Pregnancies

Carol J. Garrett

As DISCUSSED in earlier chapters, teenage pregnancy greatly accelerated during the 1950s and 1960s and hit a peak in the 1970s. The educational response to the problem during the initial phase was to exclude the pregnant student from school or, at worst (from the school's perspective), to provide home-based instruction (Ambrose, 1975). As a result, a high proportion of pregnant girls dropped out of school (Foltz, Klerman, & Jekel, 1972).

The girl who drops out of school is unlikely to finish her education and is likely to remain unmarried, unemployed, and on welfare and subsequently have a second and third child (Jekel, Klerman, & Bancroft, 1973). In turn, the teen's infant is at greater risk of death before the first birthday, and, if it survives, the infant is more likely to be classified as handicapped by the time it is of school age (Nye, 1977).

In light of the consequences to both mother and infant of teenage pregnancy, programs have been designed to meet the unique needs of the pregnant adolescent. These programs vary in their basic goals and settings and in the nature of intervention conducted. Programs have been developed in hospitals, homes, special clinics, special schools, and regular school settings. Many programs attempt to treat the girl after she has become pregnant or just after the birth of her child. Other programs are preventive and attempt to teach childrearing and/or birth control and make available birth control devices and information. Still others attempt to introduce, before pregnancy, ideas about the responsibility of childrearing and bearing to both the prospective teen father and teen mother. This chapter examines the major types of programs designed to respond to the problem of teenage pregnancy.

HOSPITAL-BASED PROGRAMS

Given the widely held policy of schools in the 1950s and 1960s to expel the pregnant teenager, social agencies were left to respond to the increase in teenage births (Anastasiow, 1982). Hospital personnel found themselves delivering low birth weight and premature infants to girls who were themselves children. One such setting was the University of Cincinnati Department of Pediatrics. Alarmed at the number of teenagers delivering, the department called on the Department of Social Work and Psychology to help develop a program for teenage mothers (Badger, 1977, 1980). Under the direction of Earladeen Badger, the Cincinnati General Hospital Infant Stimulation/Mother Training Project has become one of the most prominent hospital-based programs for teenage mothers. The program is based on the recognition of the "mutually reinforcing nature of health and educational intervention in maximizing the potential of high-risk infants, as well as the importance of early maternal-infant attachment" (Badger, Burns, & Rhoads, 1976). The target population for this project is adolescent girls giving birth at Cincinnati General and living within close proximity to the hospital. The majority of the girls are inner-city blacks and white Appalachians. A program representative visits new mothers in the hospital on the second or third postpartum day and encourages them to enroll in the program. Although the project has found that most mothers enroll readily, additional incentives include: ability to earn high school credit for class attendance, transportation pools, pictures of their infants, and free toys and educational materials. A class of 15 is recruited. Classes begin when the infant is 3 to 5 weeks old, a time when the mother's enchantment with the newborn and with mothering may be diminishing and when she may be particularly receptive to intervention (Badger et al., 1976). Classes are held weekly until the infant is 6 months old for a total of 18 to 22 sessions.

The staff involved in each class includes a "leader-instructor" (generally an early-education specialist or a pediatric nurse), a co-leader (graduate, medical, and nursing students), and a "recorder-observer." Because the classes take place in the hospital, medical services for mother and infant are readily available.

The class curriculum includes information on health and well-baby care, nutrition, and infant stimulation. Health and well-baby care emphasize preventive health care—the need for appropriate immunizations and the recognition of and appropriate responses to colds, fevers, allergies, and rashes. Nutrition information includes establishing a feeding pattern, the importance of cuddling the infant while feeding, and the introduction of solid foods. In the early sessions, infant stimulation is presented by demonstrating (either live or through films) what an infant is capable of at a given developmental stage, what purpose the behavior serves, and how the mother can encourage the acquisition of an age-appropriate skill.

The infant stimulation curriculum is designed to emphasize the importance of interaction, appropriate response to infant vocalization and signs of distress, observation of infant behavior to facilitate choice of appropriate play materials, and the sequence of developmental skills. Throughout the sessions, the importance of the mother's interaction with her infant is stressed, demonstrated, and reinforced (Badger, 1977).

An extensive hospital program for adolescent mothers has been developed in San Francisco (Grady, 1975). The program includes special service centers for the pregnant adolescent located in hospitals and two maternity homes. The centers are open to any young mother in San Francisco city and county. Services provided include formal academic education, health education, family planning counseling, home economics information, remedial reading instruction, group and individual counseling, and pre- and postnatal care. Some girls complete their high school education at a center; others return to their regular school. Two teachers and a social worker are on duty at each center. The centers share the services of remedial reading teachers, home economists, and academic and vocational counselors. Attempts are made to involve the infant's father as well as the parents and grandparents of the young parents. A nursery is available for the infants. The author reports reduced incidences of low birth weight, prematurity, obstetrical complications, and repeat pregnancies.

A comprehensive teenage maternity program was also established at San Francisco General Hospital in 1969 (Goldstein, Zalar, Grady, & Smith, 1973). The program provides adolescent girls between 16 to 21 years of age and primarily from ghetto families with vocational education, parenting skills, general guidance, and the opportunity to obtain a high school diploma or its equivalent. Medical care includes information concerning family planning, abortion, labor anesthesia, delivery, nutrition, and child development, particularly the use of discipline. The educational component of the program contains a "bare bones" curriculum with heavy attention to basic skills. Great emphasis is placed on vocational education. Social services are available to the girl and her family.

The Young Parents Program at Columbia Presbyterian Hospital in New York City is also a hospital-based program that serves adolescent mothers and fathers (Abbott, 1977; Graham, 1977). The staff consists of nurses, midwives, social workers, and pediatric nurse practitioners. The program includes a prenatal clinic, prenatal counseling, childbirth preparation, a postpartum clinic (including birth control counseling), an adolescent parenting group, and a well-baby clinic.

Abbott (1977) and Graham (1977) were both concerned with the negative attitude the professional staff had toward the pregnant teenager. A unique feature of their program was the considerable amount of training that focused on the professional staff, particularly the physician, in an attempt to modify the negative value judgment toward the sexually active teenager. It should be kept in mind that most social agencies, including the schools, have responded to the pregnant teenager on a good–bad continuum rather than viewing the girl as caught up in massive societal and physiological change.

Other hospital programs have used special clinics set up for the teenage population. One of the most prominent of these programs is at the Goldfarb Adult Development Clinic in Houston, Texas (Smith, Wait, Mumford, Nenny, & Hollins, 1978). The goals of the program are to provide: 1) comprehensive psychosocial medical care during and after delivery, 2) general education, 3) education for parenthood, and 4) motivation to pursue educational and vocational goals. The staff includes obstetricians, pediatricians, a nutritionist, registered nurses, a home economist, a social worker, and members of the Junior League of Houston. Services offered from the seventh month of pregnancy include an obstetrical examination, "information on nutrition, contraception, child development, labor preparation, and the psychosocial aspects of pregnancy" (Smith et al., 1978). Following delivery, and while still in the hospital, girls attend individual and group counseling sessions twice per day, in which child development, personal hygiene, and contraception are emphasized. As an adjunct to this program, a crisis hotline has been established. Upon leaving the program, each mother is given phone numbers of a nurse and an assistant who can be reached at any time (Smith, Mumford, & Hamner, 1975).

A variation of the center-based program has been established by Field and colleagues (Field, Widmayer, Stringer, & Ignatoff, 1980). The program is home based and meets with the mother on a biweekly basis. Participants are 150 black lower-class mothers who are either less than 19 years old or 20 to 29 years of age and who have had either full-term or premature babies. Home visits of approximately one half-hour are made biweekly by both a trained interventionist and a black, teenage work-study student. The goals of the intervention program are to educate the young mothers on child development and caregiving, to teach age-appropriate sensorimotor and cognitive exercises to the mothers, and to facilitate mother-child interaction. A group of approximately five exercises in the sensorimotor, caregiving, and interaction areas are presented.

As the number of teenage pregnancies has increased, schools have been forced by court action, civil rights, and community pressure to establish some type of program for the pregnant adolescent. Exclusions that had been supported in large part by the values of a community had to give way (Washington, 1975). As shall be seen, the changes have varied in program content and location.

SPECIAL SCHOOLS

Programs have been established in special schools either separated physically from the regular school or in the regular school itself. Many arguments have been advanced in support of the special school program (Holmes, Klerman, & Gabrielson, 1970). The program can span 12 months, with no interruption for the summer vacation. Programming is individualized, and small class size—often associated with increased academic achievement—can be maintained. The curriculum can be designed to fulfill the special needs of the pregnant adolescent, and vocational and social counseling can be made available. A lunch program that enhances the nutritional intake of the pregnant student can be provided. The father of the infant can be drawn into contact with service providers (Washington, 1975). Special school programs are said to improve attitudes toward school and to raise self-esteem among the early teen population at risk for pregnancy (Holmes et al., 1970).

One special school program often referred to as a model for other programs is at the Polly T. McCabe Center in New Haven, Connecticut (Foltz et al., 1972; Holmes et al., 1970). The program, started in 1966, serves 7th to 12th grade students 5 days per week from 9:00 a.m. to 12:00 p.m. and follows the regular school calendar. Its services are available to all pregnant teenagers in New Haven, regardless of where they seek prenatal care. After delivery, students are encouraged to return to McCabe for a time and then to rejoin their regular school. If the girl is over 16 and not school oriented, McCabe will counsel her about such alternative programs as vocational training or a high school equivalency program. The major component of the McCabe program is education. Teachers maintain contact with the regular school program and use the same texts that are used in the regular school. Classroom work is parallel to that in the regular school in the hope that the student can be integrated with a minimum of difficulty. Health counseling, medical, and social service programs are available primarily from the Young Mothers Program of Yale/New Haven Hospital (Foltz et al., 1972; Holmes et al., 1970).

The Educational Services for School-Age Parents (ESSP) program was started in New Brunswick, New Jersey, in 1969 under the auspices of the public schools (Bennett & Bardon, 1977). Services are provided both pre- and postpartum to pregnant school-age girls at the Family Learning Center. Girls may remain at the center after delivery or return to their regular school. The students continue their regular education while receiving medical, counseling, and academic assistance.

Another frequently cited special school-based program is the Young Mothers Education Development (YMED) program in Syracuse and Onondaga County, New York (Osofsky & Osofsky, 1970). School-age mothers (average age: 16 years) in the program are generally nonwhite and poor. Duration of stay in the program is flexible, in keeping with the originators' philosophy that such a program must be highly individualized. An interdisciplinary staff provides services. The facility has rooms for classes, social and psychological services, a kitchen and cafeteria, medical facilities for examinations and observation, and a nursery for infants. The nursery was provided in order to allow mothers to attend classes after delivery, care for their infants, and learn appropriate techniques of child care.

Two other comprehensive, special school-based programs similar to those described above are the Edgar Allen Poe School in Baltimore, Maryland, and the Teen Mother Program in Santa Ana, California (Dohrmann, 1979; Stine & Kelley, 1970).

The Parent/Child Program at Boothe Memorial Home, Oakland, California, is a special, residential school (Benas, 1975). A "child-mother" at Boothe is defined as 18 years of age or younger, generally on welfare, and separated from outside support, for a variety of reasons. Approximately one-half of the girls are from ethnic-minority groups. The pregnant adolescent may decide to relinquish or keep her child and has the option to remain at Boothe until she has either finished her education or gained adequate job skills. A mother could possibly remain in the program for 4 to 5 years. The Boothe program rests on the extended family concept—providing for the needs of both mother and infant and viewing them as equal in terms of service needs. Both mother and child are provided with all basic necessary services, including room, board, medical care, and educational and recreational opportunities. Upon entering the program, the mother agrees to an educational or vocational program for herself and to enroll the baby in the infant nursery. Mothers are free to visit the nursery at any time and are required to take part in the nursery's training program.

The nursery has an extensive developmental program that is presented to mothers in educational units covering such topics as diapering, feeding, and toilet training. After each baby has been observed and developmentally tested, a "play prescription" is given to the mother, which will help her maximize her infant's growth and development.

In recent years, some school systems have become less punitive in their view of the pregnant school girl and have established programs to meet the needs of these students within the regular school program on the regular school campus (Washington, 1975).

REGULAR SCHOOL PROGRAMS

A comprehensive, interdisciplinary program, begun in 1973, has been offered in three inner-city high schools in St. Paul, Minnesota, by the St. Paul Maternal and Infant Care (MIC) project (Alton, 1979). Components of the program include prenatal care, family planning, well-child care, total health care, and a day-care center for infants. The staff includes an obstetrician, adolescent medical fellow, pediatric nurse associate, social worker, dental hygienist, nutritionist, and health educator. A 3-semester parenting course, open to all students, covers such topics as "first years of a baby's life" and "family life and human sexuality." Babies of the teenagers are given learning opportunities and intellectual stimulation at the day-care center to enhance growth and development. All mothers are required, and fathers are encouraged, to take a course on child care, child development, and parenting skills. Pregnant students are evaluated for nutritional difficulties, given appropriate education and counseling, and followed postnatally.

Another school model is seen in the Maternal and Infant Care Project at Grady Memorial Hospital, Atlanta, Georgia, which has initiated the placement in three public schools of a comprehensive service program for pregnant adolescents (Klein, 1975). Nurses, counselors, and social workers are on site in the schools, although comprehensive health care is still provided at the hospital. The daily "reproductive health class" has now become coeducational and open to all students. For 15 to 16 months postpartum, services are provided at the Interconceptional Care Clinic by staff nurses, counselors, psychologists, and physicians. Similar school programs operate in Maryland (Dohrmann, 1979), New Jersey (Bennett & Bardon, 1977), and California (Stine & Kelley, 1970).

These comprehensive school programs attempt to maintain the regular academic program as well as to provide vocational training, health counseling, medical services, mental health counseling, well-baby care, and child-rearing. They are, in the main, designed for the pregnant teen or young parent. Other programs that have been designed to prevent pregnancy or to prepare young people for parenthood are described below.

OTHER APPROACHES

Attempts to ameliorate the teenage pregnancy problem have included a variety of efforts supported by the March of Dimes (MOD) and the program funded by the newly created Office of Adolescent Pregnancy Programs (OAPP), Education for Parenthood (EFP). Preventive programs, such as those offered by Planned Parenthood, have also been initiated.

OAPP supports efforts to deal with adolescent pregnancy through the provision of grants, technical assistance, and evaluation (Nix, 1980). Funded projects are required to provide 10 core services: pregnancy testing and maternity counseling, family planning services, primary and preventive health services, nutrition information and counseling, referral for screening and treatment of venereal disease, referral to pediatric care, educational services in sexuality and family life, referral to educational and vocational services, adoption counseling and referral, and referral to other appropriate health services. Supplemental services that are encouraged but not required include child care, consumer education and homemaking, counseling for the extended family, and transportation. Counseling/social services are to be integrated into all core services. Projects can take the form of single-site, linked, rural, statewide, countywide, citywide, or research programs. Several of these formats may be integrated in a single project (Office of Adolescent Pregnancy Programs Information Bulletin [OAPPIB], 1980). Four projects were funded in 1979: Addison County Parent/Child Center, Middlebury, Vermont; Teenage Maternity Project of Florence Crittenton Services, Houston, Texas; Family Planning Services of Central Massachusetts, Worcester, Massachusetts; and Adolescent Pregnancy Care and Prevention Program, the Bronx, New York.

The Addison County Parent/Child Center is located in a poor, rural county and uses outreach workers who have successfully raised children themselves and who preferably have teaching and/or counseling experience. These workers act as advocates, teachers, and case managers for the pregnant teenagers and their families. The program plans to coordinate existing services (i.e., public health nursing, community mental health, child care, and Planned Parenthood) and will add new services (i.e., infant and toddler programs, pregnancy prevention programs, and parenting classes). The immediate objectives of the project are to reduce the incidence of pregnancy and repeat pregnancy among the adolescent population and "to improve the health, emotional, educational, and social status of adolescent mothers and their children" (OAPPIB, 1980). Ultimate goals of the project are to reduce child abuse, maternal/infant mortality, birth defects, second pregnancies, school dropout, and the number of welfare recipients.

The Teenage Maternity Project (TMP) of Florence Crittenton Services in Houston, Texas, proposes to reduce the incidence of adolescent pregnancy, to increase responsibility in teenage sexual behavior, and to involve the community more fully in support services and linkages. This project allows for the continuation of an existing program that has the cooperation and support of the public schools, the health department, and the United Way (OAPPIB, 1980).

The Worcester Adolescent Pregnancy Program of Family Planning Services of Central Massachusetts has estimated that it will serve 150 clients, 13 to 17 years of age, in the greater Worcester area. Its goals are to develop a citywide network of services (emphasizing accessibility and availability), to maximize the utilization of existing services, to develop expertise in the management of pregnant adolescents, to promote the desirability to teens of a service network, and to supervise and ensure the quality of such a network. Although Family Planning Services of Central Massachusetts, in existence for the past 3 years, has focused on family planning services, it has been expanded to provide many other types of counseling, a "hot line," and rap groups, as well as services to parents and professionals, the intent being to provide pre- and postnatal care and to coordinate existing services. The sites include two hospitals and the Family Health and Social Service Center (OAPPIB, 1980).

The Adolescent Pregnancy Care and Prevention Program (TAPCAPP) in the Bronx, New York, is targeted at poor adolescents of primarily black and Puerto Rican backgrounds. The project expects to serve approximately 300 teenagers in the first year. An innovative component of the program is the inclusion of "Big Sisters" as primary contacts with clients in the hope of reaping the benefits of close personal attention. In addition to core services, the project plans to provide nursery care, an "arts encounter" program, camping experience, academic tutoring, a pregnancy and sexuality "hot line," transportation, and a community education component (OAPPIB, 1980).

The National Foundation–March of Dimes (MOD) has been active in addressing the issues of risks associated with adolescent pregnancy. It supports the Houston Solution Committee, co-sponsors the Institute on Education for Responsible Childbearing, and supports the development of numerous informational and educational publications. The latter include "How to Help Children Become Better Parents: A Resource Kit for Parents and Community Leaders Who Wish to Introduce Education for Parenthood into Their Schools," produced in conjunction with the National Parent-Teacher Association, and "Healthy Babies: Chance or Choice," developed in cooperation with the Future Homemakers of America. MOD has also funded the development by Bank Street College of the Preparenthood Education Program (Boeghold & Hooks, 1978). The program presents information on pregnancy, child growth, and nutrition in an easy-to-read, often comic-book format in both English and Spanish. MOD has fully supported the Educational Development Corporation's Starting a Healthy Family program, which is a comprehensive educational program composed of separate materials for high school students and their parents.

In addition to supporting the development and dissemination of educational materials, MOD actively supports numerous programs for pregnant adolescents across the nation (see material available from the National Foundation–March of Dimes, 1275 Mamaroneck Ave., White Plains, NY 10605).

A major program aimed at the overall teenage population is Education for Parenthood (EFP) (Kinch & Kruger, 1970; Morris, 1977). The program was launched in 1972 with the following goals: to teach the adolescent about child development; the social, emotional, and medical needs of children; the role of families in socialization and development; and factors in prenatal and neonatal development; to give youth experience with young children; to answer questions about parenthood and the young child; and to prepare youth for possible careers in working with young children (Morris, 1977). It was for the EFP program that the Educational Development Corporation's Exploring Childhood Curriculum was first developed. For children in grades 7 to 12, it utilizes class instruction as well as practical experience. The second phase of the EFP program, after curriculum development, was the granting of support to voluntary youth-serving organizations to develop and implement programs. The recipients of these funds were: the Boy Scouts of America, Boys' Clubs of America, National 4-H Clubs of America, Girl Scouts of the U.S.A., National Federation of Settlements and Neighborhood Centers, Salvation Army, and Save the Children Federation (Morris, 1977).

The Boy Scouts of America program emphasized child care as a possible career. Explorer Scouts had the opportunity for field work in addition to class instruction. Seminars on family dynamics and children were offered.

The Boys' Clubs of America (BCA) had programs in 20 sites serving 1,000 participants by its third year. Students in grades 10 through 12 were evenly divided by sex. The majority was white. The core concept of the BCA program was "Help-a-Kid." Its goals were to enhance self-knowledge and knowledge of others (particularly the young child), to increase awareness of the importance of family influence, to gain an understanding of the responsibilities of parenthood, to broaden knowledge of those factors affecting child development, to explore careers in working with children, and to learn skills for working with the young child.

The National 4-H Club Foundation of America had programs in four geographical areas, serving primarily white females in grades 10 through 12. The goals of the program were: to enhance self-knowledge and understanding of parenting and adult roles; to increase knowledge of alternative and traditional family styles, of prenatal and child development, and of the behavior and development of normal and handicapped children; to improve human relations skills; to learn about pregnancy, conception, and contraception; and to provide field experience.

The Girl Scouts of the U.S.A. established EFP programs in 200 councils nationwide. Participants were primarily white girls in grades 6 through 9. Goals were to increase knowledge of child development and family life and to enhance adolescent self-awareness and growth. Information was presented primarily in a learning-by-doing format. Girls gained experience in situations as varied as working as an aide in a day camp to babysitting for handicapped persons.

The National Federation of Settlements and Neighborhood Centers developed the program Preparing Teenagers for Parenthood (PTP). Its target population was high-risk youth—low income, young (mean age: 13.6 years), predominantly black. Participants were evenly divided by sex and were in grades 6 through 9. Objectives were to enhance self-concept, improve language skills, enhance insight and reality testing abilities, develop interpersonal skills, and improve decision-making abilities. All PTP programs included education in human sexuality and in the medical, social, and emotional aspects of pregnancy and childbirth. Field work was provided. The overall emphasis was on child development.

The Salvation Army's EFP program served primarily females in grades 10 through 12. Many girls, from a variety of ethnic origins, were of low income, and 37% of them lived in a Salvation Army setting. All programs encouraged self-awareness and provided some practicum experience with young children. Knowledge of child development and of the responsibilities and obligations of parenthood were stressed.

The Save the Children Federation's Teenagers As Child Advocates (TACA) program was targeted at rural Appalachia. The average age of participants was 13.4 years. Most were white females in grades 6 through 9. The program, which recruited and paid recent or potential school dropouts, included instruction in child development, child-care techniques, and family life. Participants were given practical experience working in child-care centers as well as with individual families.

A survey (Morris, 1977) of the seven organizations supported by EFP has indicated that child development was the subject they most emphasized, followed by self-awareness and sex education. The majority of the trainers were EFP staff, although paid and nonpaid resource persons were also used. Training approaches, in order of most to least frequently utilized, were: group discussion, rap sessions, lectures, audio-visual aides, demonstration and role playing, skill development, observation of children, and caring for children. The majority of sessions took place at the organization site, but use of community facilities, particularly schools, was also frequent.

CONTRACEPTIVE INFORMATION

Many professionals feel that, given the trend for adolescents to become sexually active at earlier ages and given a new, more accepting attitude toward sexually active teenagers, the best approach to preventing premature and unwanted pregnancy is to make contraceptive information and supplies available to those teenagers (Rocky Mountain Planned Parenthood, 1979–1980). Of the 4 million 15- to 19-year olds and the 375,000 13- to 14-year-olds who were at risk of unintended pregnancy in 1975, 1.6 million received no contraceptive services. It is estimated that 37% used no contraceptive method whatsoever (Dryfoos, 1978). As the adolescent becomes older, he or she is more likely to receive services. Of the at-risk 18- to 19-year-olds, 33% received such services, compared with only 3% to 4% of the 13- to 14-year-olds. The low-income teenager was more likely to be served. Dryfoos (1978) has suggested that teenagers will avail themselves of contraceptive information and services if provided to them. While the setting for such services need not be unique to the adolescent, confidentiality and convenience are necessary inducements. Breakstone (1979) has found that 50% of the adolescents included in her study used contraceptives consistently and that schools were the best source of information on the subject. She also found that less than one-third of sexually active teenagers had used contraception on the occasion of first intercourse. The Alan Guttmacher Institute (1976) has reported that four out of five sexually active teenagers had had unprotected intercourse at some time and that even those who used contraceptives were likely to choose the least effective methods.

What is the reason for the failure of teenagers to use appropriate contraceptive methods? The Alan Guttmacher Institute has surmised that the basic reasons are the ignorance of teenagers and the inaccessibility of services. Others (Tyrer & Josimovich, 1977) have cited as contributing factors the lack of education and services, fear of lack of "spontaneity" or of being considered promiscuous, fear of lack of confidentiality, and cost of contraceptive services. Reasons described by teenagers themselves include the reluctance to communicate with parents, impersonality of birth control education, necessity of revealing sexual activity, "hassles" by doctors and pharmacists, lack of spontaneity, cost, and parents finding out (Clinkscales & Gallo, 1977). Clinkscales and Gallo (1977) have also cited the assumed benefits of pregnancy, which include status as a mother, proof of "womanhood," attention, the thrill of risk-taking, and independence.

It is felt that, in the past, fear of parental disapproval and legal repercussions has discouraged the development of programs to educate teenagers on contraceptive methods and provide them with those methods if necessary. Wilcox and McAnarney (1975) and Scales (1979) have reported, however, that the great majority of parents support the offering of sex education courses in the schools and the provision of contraceptives for sexually active adolescents.

A list of exemplary programs focusing on contraceptive information follows: Rocky Mountain Planned Parenthood (Denver) offers, without regard to age or marital status, services including medical services and counseling on methods of birth control, laboratory tests, pelvic examinations, PAP smears, and contraceptive supplies; pregnancy counseling for problem pregnancies; abortion counseling; continuing education for involved professionals; community education (including high schools); referrals; and publications targeted at young persons (Rocky Mountain Planned Parenthood, 1979–80).

The multidisciplinary staff of the Youth Clinic Program in Los Angeles offers free medical care and supplies, as well as psychosocial counseling, in an atmosphere of absolute confidentiality. Group discussion is used heavily, while individual counseling is also available. Every opportunity is taken to offer contraceptive information. Abortion and postabortion counseling and referral are also available. And, an outreach program is offered to schools. Minkowski, Weiss, Lowther, Shonick, and Heidbreder (1974) have found that, indeed, their heaviest caseload is with the nonpregnant adolescent.

Hendricks (1977) has described The Door—a comprehensive multiservice center for adolescents in Manhattan. Components of the program (all provided free of charge) include family planning counseling, sex education, pre- and postnatal instruction, and nutritional counseling. The center has its own laboratory and pharmacy. Mental health services, in addition to legal, vocational, and educational counseling, are provided, along with a learning center to assist adolescents with academic problems. Participants also have access to performing arts, dance, theater, music, and graphic art programs. It is estimated that The Door serves approximately 350 adolescents per day. The majority of participants are black or Hispanic, living independently, and 16 years of age or older.

The Comprehensive Adolescent Clinic in Baltimore offers medical and dental care, emotional and psychological support, and education (including contraceptive information) in health care. Services are provided by a multidisciplinary team, which includes social workers, pediatricians, gynecologists, obstetricians, dentists, public health nurses, psychologists, and psychiatrists (Finkelstein, 1972).

Several individuals and organizations have found peer counseling a successful approach. Scales (1979), for example, has reported on the success of the Teenage Health Consultants project in five Minneapolis clinics. Since 1972, 100 young persons have been trained to provide education (including sex education) to their peers. Parental involvement is stressed. It is estimated that 5,000 youths have been reached by this program to date. Vadies (1977) has supported the said value of peers in informing, referring, and educating.

The Future Homemakers of America, in cooperation with the March of Dimes, has produced a workbook for peer educators entitled "Healthy Babies: Chance or Choice." The workbook provides information on birth defects, facts on and project possibilities for teenage pregnancy, nutrition, drug use/abuse, and infection. It also makes suggestions for bringing about change (impact, needs assessment, getting help, using special occasions) and for effective communication techniques (talks, rap sessions, skits/puppets, displays, printed materials, audio-visual aids, mass media). It is estimated that 2,000,000 teenagers have been reached since 1975 by the peer educators and their advisors who have made use of this workbook. Success has been reported in individual, citywide, and statewide projects.

Marnet (1977) has reported on a high school program that uses peer counselors in Washington, D.C., wherein Planned Parenthood provides support and supervision for the Teen Health Center at the school. In existence since January 1975, the center offers rap sessions, gynecological examinations, all birth control methods, pregnancy testing, "problem pregnancy" counseling, and venereal disease testing. Planned Parenthood also provides peer counselor training. The staff consists of a director, receptionist, nurse, mental health specialist, school social worker, and peer counselors. The center is a cooperative effort of Planned Parenthood, the Department of Human Resources, and the school.

The pediatrician, Wilcox and McAnarney (1975) have argued, may be the best agent of intervention in adolescent pregnancy. They believe that the developmental and preventive specialty, in combination with the role as primary physician, make the pediatrician a good provider of family planning and sex education services for his or her teenage patients. As yet, however, no information has been collected on either the number of young persons who use their pediatrician in this way or the efficacy of this approach.

Regardless of the type of assistance the sexually active adolescent may take, it is clear that there is a great need to provide it. Smith (1981) has suggested ways to minimize community resistance to these services and maximize their use by the target population. Smith recommends responsible, nonsensational media coverage that stresses the common needs of the age group rather than the unique needs of the already sexually active or pregnant teenager. Using laymen in the planning and implementation process is helpful to defuse resistance. To encourage the use of services, Smith (1981) suggests the basics of "accessibility, convenience, confidentiality, and affordability." Further, services other than those of family planning should be offered. Those offered can be made known through radio announcements, school nurses and counselors, peer recommendations, and brochures.

REFERENCES

Abbott, M. I. 1977. The teen is pregnant: What happens now? Paper presented at the 108th Convention of the American Public Health Association, October, Los Angeles, Calif.

Alan Guttmacher Institute. 1976. Eleven Million Teenagers: What Can Be Done About the Epidemic of Adolescent Pregnancies in the United States? Alan Guttmacher Institute, New York.

Alton, I. R. 1979. Nutrition services for pregnant adolescents within a public high school. Journal of the American Dietetic Association 74:667–669.

Ambrose, L. 1975. Discrimination persists against pregnant students remaining in school. Family Planning/Population Reporter 4(1):10–13.

Anastasiow, N. J. 1982. Preparing adolescents in childrearing: Before and after pregnancy. In: M. Sugar (ed.), Adolescent Parenthood. Spectrum Pub. Inc., Jamaica, N.Y.

Badger, E. 1977. The Infant Stimulation/Mother Training Project. In: B. Caldwell and D. Stedman (eds.), Infant Education, pp. 45–62. Walker Publishing Co., New York.

Badger, E. 1980. Effects of parent education programs on teenage mothers and their offspring. In: S. Harel (ed.), The At Risk Infant. Excerpta Medica, Amsterdam.
Badger, E., Burns, D., and Rhoads, B. 1976. Education for adolescent mothers in a hospital setting. American Journal of Public Health 66:469–472.
Benas, E. 1975. Residential care of the child-mother and her infant. Child Welfare 54(4):290–294.
Bennett, V. C., and Bardon, J. I. 1977. The effects of a school program on teenage mothers and their children. American Journal of Orthopsychiatry 47:671–678.
Boeghold, B. D., and Hooks, W. D. (eds.). 1978. The Bank Street College of the Preparenthood Education Program. National Foundation–March of Dimes, Mamaroneck, N.Y.
Breakstone, J. 1979. Survey of Decision Making on Contraceptive Usage Among Teenagers. Summary Report. Alameda County Family Planning Forum, Oakland, Calif.
Clinkscales, K., and Gallo, J. 1977. How teens see it. In: D. J. Bogue (ed.), Adolescent Fertility: The Proceedings of an International Conference. Community and Family Study Center, University of Chicago, Chicago.
Dohrmann, H. 1979. Nutrition education in the Santa Ana Teen Mother Program. Journal of the American Dietetic Association 74:665–667.
Dryfoos, J. G. 1978. The incidence and outcome of adolescent pregnancy in the United States. In: A. S. Parkes, R. V. Short, M. Potts, and M. Herbertson (eds.), Fertility in Adolescence, pp. 85–100. Galton Foundation, Cambridge, England.
Field, T., Widmayer, S., Stringer, S., and Ignatoff, E. 1980. An intervention and developmental follow-up of preterm infants born to teenage, lower-class mothers, pp. 29–33. In: S. Harel (ed.), The At Risk Infant. Excerpta Medica, Amsterdam.
Finkelstein, R. 1972. Program for the sexually active teenager. Pediatrics Clinics of North America 19:791–795.
Foltz, A. M., Klerman, L., and Jekel, J. 1972. Pregnancy and special education: Who stays in school? American Journal of Public Health 62(12):1612–1619.
Goldstein, P. J., Zalar, M. K., Grady, E. W., and Smith, R. W. 1973. Vocational education: An unusual approach to adolescent pregnancy. Journal of Reproductive Medicine 10:77–79.
Grady, E. W. 1975. Models of comprehensive service—Hospital based. Journal of School Health 45:268.
Graham, E. 1977. Medical responsibilities. In: D. J. Bogue (ed.), Adolescent Fertility: The Proceedings of an International Conference. Community and Family Study Center, University of Chicago, Chicago.
Healthy babies: Chance or choice? A peer education approach. March of Dimes, 1275 Mamaroneck Ave., White Plains, N.Y. 10605.
Hendricks, L. E. 1977. Integrated model. In: D. J. Bogue (ed.), Adolescent Fertility: The Proceedings of an International Conference. Community and Family Study Center, University of Chicago, Chicago.
Holmes, M. E., Klerman, L. V., and Gabrielson, I. W. 1970. A new approach to educational services for the pregnant student. Journal of School Health 40:168–172.
Jekel, J. F., Klerman, L. V., and Bancroft, D. R. E. 1973. Factors associated with rapid subsequent pregnancies among school-age mothers. American Journal of Public Health 63:769–773.
Kinch, R. A., and Kruger, E. 1970. Some sociomedical aspects on the adolescent pregnancy. International Journal of Gynecology/Obstetrics 8:840.
Klein, L. 1975. Models of comprehensive service—regular school based. Journal of School Health 45:271–273.

Marnet, L. 1977. School setting model. In: D. J. Bogue (ed.), Adolescent Fertility: The Proceedings of an International Conference. Community and Family Study Center, University of Chicago, Chicago.

Minkowski, W. L., Weiss, R. C., Lowther, L., Shonick, H., and Heidbreder, G. A. 1974. Family planning services for adolescents and young adults. The Western Journal of Medicine 120:116–123.

Morris, L. A. (ed.). 1977. Education for parenthood: A program, curriculum, and evaluation guide. U.S. Department of Health, Education, and Welfare publication (ODHS) 77-30125, Washington, D.C.

Nix, L. M. 1980. Adolescent pregnancy: Problems, programs, and new directions. Office of Adolescent Pregnancy Programs, U.S. Department of Health, Education, and Welfare, Washington, D.C.

Nye, F. I. 1977. School-Age Parenthood: Consequences for Babies, Mothers, Fathers, Etc. Extension Bulletin 667. Washington State University, Pullman, Wash.

Office of Adolescent Pregnancy Programs Information Bulletin. 1980. 1:1–14.

Osofsky, H. J., and Osofsky, J. D. 1970. Adolescents as mothers: Results of a program for low-income pregnant teenagers with some emphasis upon infants' development. American Journal of Orthopsychiatry 40:825–834.

Rocky Mountain Planned Parenthood Services, 1979/80. 2030 East 20th Ave., Denver, Colo. 80205.

Scales, P. 1979. The context of sex education and the reduction of teenage pregnancy. Child Welfare 58:263–273.

Smith, P. B. 1981. Reproductive health care for teens. In: M. Sugar (ed.), Adolescent Parenthood. Spectrum, New York.

Smith, P. B., Mumford, D. M., and Hamner, E. 1975. Hotline for teenage mothers. American Journal of Nursing 75:1504.

Smith, P. B., Wait, R. B., Mumford, D. M., Nenny, S. W., and Hollins, B. T. 1978. The medical impact of an ante-partum program for pregnant adolescents: A statistical analysis. American Journal of Public Health 68:169–172.

Stine, O. C., and Kelley, E. B. 1970. Evaluation of a school for young mothers: The frequency of prematurity among infants born to mothers under 17 years of age according to the mother's attendance of a special school during pregnancy. Pediatrics 46:581–587.

Tyrer, L. B., and Josimovich, J. 1977. Contraception in teenagers. Clinical Obstetrics and Gynecology 20:651–663.

Vadies, G. 1977. Peer counseling model. In: D. J. Bogue (ed.), Adolescent Fertility: The Proceedings of an International Conference. Community and Family Study Center, University of Chicago, Chicago.

Washington, V. E. 1975. Models of comprehensive service—Special school based. Journal of School Health 45:274–277.

Wilcox, A. J., and McAnarney, E. R. 1975. The pediatrician and the primary prevention of adolescent pregnancy. Clinical Pediatrics 14(3):226–231.

7

Preparing Adolescents for Parenthood
Does It Make a Difference?

Allan Shwedel

BEING A PARENT can be difficult, especially for an adolescent. Being a young child can be difficult, especially for the child of an adolescent. In an effort to minimize the difficulties and potentially negative consequences resulting from teenage pregnancy and parenthood, agencies at the local, state, and national levels have been providing a wide array of educational, medical, psychological, and occupational services to pregnant adolescents, adolescent mothers, their children, and even male and female adolescents who have no immediate plans of becoming parents. Over the past 10 years, numerous projects have been developed, services have been provided to countless teenagers, and millions of dollars have been spent. The issue examined in this chapter is the impact these diverse projects have had on the lives of their clients.

While impact can be viewed from a myriad of perspectives, the present examination is limited to the following questions:

1. Have the services resulted in improved educational or occupational opportunities for adolescent mothers?
2. Have the services resulted in improved physical, cognitive, or social functioning among the children born to adolescents?
3. Have the services resulted in an improvement in parenting skills and attitudes toward young children among participating adolescents?

Answers to these questions about project impact should enable planners to make decisions regarding the future direction of services to potential parents. In addition, identifying gaps in our ability to gather the information needed to answer these questions should serve to direct researchers in their future efforts.

In general, the data examined below come from project reports that were geared to issues and audiences deemed important by the project staff. Since negative findings tend not to occur in published reports, this review is based on data from relatively effective but not necessarily typical projects. This bias limits the generalizability of the findings; nevertheless, the major issue at this time is whether or not it is possible to document positive impact on adolescents and their children as a result of the services being provided by various public and private agencies.

IMPACT ON MOTHERS

Traditionally, pregnancy for the adolescent female has often meant the end of formal educational opportunity or, at best, placement in some type of limited, home-based educational program (Ambrose, 1975; Foltz, Klerman, & Jekel, 1972). Without a high school diploma, the adolescent mother is at a serious disadvantage in terms of obtaining financial security for herself and her child. In response to this problem, many communities have begun special classes for pregnant teenagers. Other communities have decided to encourage these teenagers to remain in their regular schools with the additional provision of medical and psychological services (Alton, 1979; Berg, Taylor, Edwards, & Hakanson, 1979). The justification for these in-school programs is that, in addition to their medical benefits, this arrangement lowers the dropout rate and provides the adolescent with a support group during a difficult period in her life. This informal support group would be composed of either other pregnant adolescents or the teenager's current friends at school.

Educational programming data strongly suggest that in-school programs do increase the likelihood that adolescent mothers will continue their education at least through the completion of high school. Educational Services for School Age Parents (ESSP), an in-school comprehensive educational and medical program in New Brunswick, New Jersey, has been described by Bennett and Bardon (1977). In New Brunswick prior to 1969, pregnant adolescents were served via a home-based program. From 1962 to 1969, every pregnant girl dropped out of the home-based program and, in effect, dropped out of school. The in-school program began in 1969, and during the next 3 years the situation was reversed to the extent that a considerable (but unspecified) number of pregnant teenagers continued their education. More substantial evidence of the impact of the ESSP program comes from data comparing the amount of schooling among the project participants and a comparison group created on a post hoc basis. The project group completed significantly more formal schooling after delivery than did the comparison-group mothers.

Alton (1979) has reported that 85% of the pregnant adolescents in an in-school program in St. Paul, Minnesota, completed high school. Link (1979) has likewise reported that 80% of the students in a special in-school class for pregnant adolescents in Lafayette, Louisiana, completed their educational program and were generally employed. In both cases, pregnancy did not result in the termination of educational opportunity for these women.

Two postpartum programs provide some preliminary comparative data. Cartoof (1978) has reported on a postpartum medical and parenting program in inner-city Boston in which 80% of the mothers returned to school after delivery. By the end of 1 year, however, 50% of the sample had dropped out of school. Goldstein, Zalar, Grady, and Smith (1973) have reported that in a hospital maternity program in San Francisco, 47% of the sample dropped out of high school after their babies were born. Differences in demographic characteristics among adolescents in these projects make it impossible to statistically compare in-school programs with postpartum programs. However, the high dropout rate among women who received postpartum services does attest to the difficulties adolescent mothers encounter in completing their high school educations.

In addition to early termination of schooling, subsequent pregnancy is another factor that affects the adolescent mother's chances of life success (Goldstein et al., 1973). Each additional child increases the drain on the mother's limited financial and emotional resources. In response to this problem of recurring pregnancy, many programs for pregnant adolescents include training in birth control techniques as an important component. The aim of birth control instruction is to decrease the incidence of repeated unplanned pregnancies.

Some projects have assessed the impact of training in this area via follow-up interviews in which former clients are asked about their use of contraceptives and subsequent pregnancies. The only true comparison data come from a study of Tatelbaum, Adams, Kash, McAnarney, Roghmann, Coulter, Charney, and Plume (1978). The focus of the study was to assess the Rochester Adolescent Maternity Project (RAMP), a multidisciplinary service program that provided medical, prenatal, psychological, and peer-group support services. They compared RAMP with a neighborhood health center that provided prenatal classes and medical services and with a hospital clinic that provided only prenatal medical services. A 1-year follow-up indicated that 17% of the hospital clients, 15% of the neighborhood clinic clients, and only 6.5% of the RAMP clients had become pregnant within the postintervention interval. In terms of contraceptive use, the figures ranged from 49% as regular users among the RAMP clients to 25% as regular users among the hospital clients.

Follow-up data from an in-school program in Syracuse, New York (Osofsky & Osofsky, 1970), have revealed that 38% of the women in the original sample of pregnant teenagers had become pregnant at least once within a 3-year interval. Cartoof (1978) has reported that within 2 years there was a 50% repeat pregnancy rate among participants in a postpartum program in Brighton, Massachusetts. Finally, in a 1-year follow-up study, Badger and Burns (1980) have found that 68.9% of the women who regularly attended postpartum classes in Cincinnati were using some form of birth control. This percentage did not differ significantly from a comparison group of women who attended postpartum classes irregularly. In terms of repeat pregnancy, however, significantly fewer regular attenders (23%) than irregular attenders (35%) had become pregnant again.

Comparing results among these projects is difficult because of the wide variability in the follow-up interval. Adequate year-by-year baseline data are lacking. It also appears that the age of the adolescent mother is a meaningful variable, one that has not been controlled for or in some cases even reported.

While baseline data are provided by Sarrel and Davis (1966), these data were collected prior to the widespread availability of birth control pills. A cohort of 15-year-olds followed by Sarrel and Davis had an average of 3.4 pregnancies per woman over a 5-year interval. The comparative data from the Tatelbaum et al. study (1978) suggest that differences among programs in terms of setting and services provided can have some impact on subsequent pregnancies. However, no studies have adequately controlled for motivational differences among groups. The data from Badger and Burns (1980) suggest that motivation may be a key variable.

Most programs for pregnant adolescents also include an educational component focusing on the new baby. This component usually deals with the nutritional and medical needs of the infant. Yet, instruction in the areas of childrearing techniques and developmental milestones is also sometimes provided. In a study of pregnant adolescents who took part in an in-school program, Bennett and Bardon (1977) have found statistically significant pre-post gains on tests of knowledge of family life and human reproduction. The Bennett and Bardon study is relatively unique, since testing for knowledge of parenting skills has not been an integral part of the assessment of programs for pregnant teenagers.

In contrast to antepartum programs, postpartum programs tend to be more concerned with child-care training. Field, Widmayer, Stringer, and Ignatoff (1980) have reported that teenage mothers who received biweekly home visits had significantly more realistic developmental expectations for their children than had mothers who received no postpartum educational services. Badger, Burns, and Rhoads (1976) have also reported pre–post gains in basic knowledge about infant health, nutrition, and development.

In-school educational programs offered to the pregnant adolescent (see, e.g., Bennett & Bardon, 1977) appear to have a positive impact on subsequent schooling, perhaps by providing important services in the context of an ongoing school setting (Link, 1979). But, in contrast to their positive impact on educational attainment, in-school programs appear less consistently successful in affecting the rate of subsequent pregnancy or contraceptive usage (Osofsky & Osofsky, 1970).

The effectiveness of in-school programs for pregnant adolescents in teaching about family life, nutrition, and child development is unclear at this time, since solely the Bennett and Bardon (1977) study has reported data from an in-school program providing instruction in these areas. Since it is the business of schools to transmit knowledge, however, it is conceivable that they could become effective disseminators of parenting information to pregnant adolescents. One question that needs to be addressed is whether knowledge gained in school prior to parenthood will transfer to actual childrearing situations or whether follow-up instruction will be needed once the child is born. The data from postpartum programs (Badger & Burns, 1980) suggest that adolescents need educational and emotional support services both before and after delivery.

To date, the occupational status of the teenage mother who has participated in a special program has not been adequately assessed. While some programs, such as the one begun at San Francisco General Hospital in 1969, have stressed vocational education (Goldstein et al., 1973), there are no reports on the success these women have had once they entered the job market. In a 1-year follow-up of postpartum parenting classes, Badger and Burns (1980) have reported that a significantly greater proportion of women who had attended classes regularly were either working or in school as compared with women who had attended irregularly. These data, however, do not separate working mothers from student mothers. Obviously, more data are needed regarding employment status and income level before an evaluation can be made of the impact of educational services for adolescent mothers on later economic security and job satisfaction.

IMPACT ON OFFSPRING

It is recognized that a child's long-term physical, cognitive, and social development is affected by both antepartum and postpartum environmental factors. Concern about teenage pregnancy derives not only from its consequences on the mother's life, therefore, but also from its impact on the child's life. For biological reasons during pregnancy and for primarily cultural reasons after birth, the mother serves as the primary mediator between the larger environment and her child. In many cases, however, the adolescent mother is unable to provide an optimal prenatal or postnatal environment. As mentioned above, programs for the adolescent mother often provide training in child-care techniques. It is assumed that this training will result in improved life chances for her children.

One way to measure the impact of an antepartum program on the life chances of the adolescent's child is by examining the frequency of obstetric complications and neonatal functioning. These variables are medical indications of risk and have been shown to correlate with the long-term medical and educational status of children. Low birth weight and prematurity are commonly used indicators of medical risk. Bennett and Bardon (1977) have reported that the incidence of low birth weight (less than 2,500 grams) nationwide is about 14.5% among infants born to teenagers. The data from a number of projects indicate that antepartum intervention can greatly decrease the incidence of low birth weight (Alton, 1979; Bennett & Bardon, 1977; Osofsky & Osofsky, 1970; Smith, Wait, Mumford, Nenney, & Hollins, 1978; Tatelbaum et al., 1978). The Bennett and Bardon data are the most impressive, with an incidence of only 1% low birth weight among infants born to participants of an in-school antepartum program, but their findings are not unique. Stine and Kelley (1970) created a post hoc comparison group and found a significantly lower incidence of low birth weight (12% vs. 24%) among infants born to mothers who attended a special school for unwed mothers versus infants born to mothers who did not. Nutrition appears as a key factor in this area, and efforts to encourage the pregnant teenager to choose her diet carefully or to actively provide her with appropriate meals have been beneficial (Alton, 1979).

Only one study has looked at the effect of antepartum classes on neonatal functioning. Smith et al. (1978) have reported that infants born to 15- and 16-year-olds who participated in special classes had significantly higher Apgar scores immediately after birth as compared with infants born to like-age teenage mothers who did not attend classes. Among infants born to 17- and 18-year-olds, however, attendance made no significant differences in Apgar scores.

In her role as primary caretaker of her child, the mother's knowledge of the child's needs and capabilities and her ability to provide the appropriate environment will also affect the child's life chances. Data from both antepartum in-school programs and postpartum hospital programs indicate that mothers can be trained to be more effective caregivers for their children. In addition to gains in basic knowledge of child care and developmental milestones, there is observational evidence that mothers use more facilitative childrearing practices as a result of both kinds of programs. Field et al. (1980) have reported that teenage mothers who participated in a program at the Mailman Center in Miami, Florida, engaged in more face-to-face interactions with their infants than did a comparison group of mothers. Badger et al. (1976) have reported that mothers became more responsive to their infants during the course of an 8-week postpartum training class. In this study, it is possible that, as the child matured, its concomitant increase in communicative ability may have affected the mother's behavior, that is, increased her reciprocal behavior. The addition of a comparison group would have provided the information necessary to assess the impact of Badger et al.'s program. Robertson (1978) has reported a frequency of facilitative language in teenage mothers who participated in a daily parent training course that was greater than in either a comparison group of mothers who received no training or in mothers who participated in only weekly training sessions. In social and emotional interaction patterns, on the other hand, Robertson (1978) found no consistent treatment effects.

The evidence from Field et al. (1980) and Badger et al. (1976) suggest that the teenage mother can be taught to modify her infant's environment. The important issue, however, is whether these changes really have a beneficial impact on the infant. In the report by Field et al. (1980), preterm infants born to teenage mothers who participated in a postpartum home instruction program scored significantly higher on the Denver Developmental Scales at 4 months of age and on the Bayley Cognitive Scale at 8 months than did a randomly assigned control group of preterm infants.

Using a post hoc comparison group, Bennett and Bardon (1977) have provided some evidence of the long-term value of an in-school program for pregnant adolescents. The researchers carried out a 1- to 5-year follow-up on children born to teenagers who had participated in the program from 1969 to 1975. On the Vineland Social Maturity Scale, the children born to mothers in the treatment group scored significantly higher than children born to mothers in the post hoc comparison group ($\bar{x}$ = 120 vs. 108). While data regarding home environment were not obtained from the comparison group, treatment group children came from households that were rated as being above the national norms on the Caldwell HOME Inventory. The treatment group children also scored above their norm group on the Caldwell Preschool Inventory.

Truss, Bensen, Hirsh, and Lickiss (1977) have reported on a 1- and 2-year follow-up of children whose teenage mothers participated in a 10- to 12-week infant/child management course. The authors report data from three different comparison groups: 1) random controls, 2) invited but did not attend, and 3) willing to be tested but could not come to class. On the Bzoch-League Receptive-Expressive Emergent Language Scale, a measure of language functioning, children in the treatment group scored at 12 months of age significantly higher than all three comparison groups on the receptive language scale and significantly higher than two of the three groups on the expressive language scale. By 24 months of age, the magnitude of the difference between the treatment group and all three comparison groups had decreased on the receptive language scale and had decreased for two of three comparison groups on the expressive language scale. At 24 months of age, four out of six of these comparisons were still statistically significant. The Caldwell HOME Inventory was administered at the 24-month follow-up. It revealed no significant between-group differences. In contrast to the authors' interpretation of these data as indicating persistent effects, the data suggest that the magnitude of the intervention effect begins to lessen as the child grows older and as the interval between intervention and follow-up testing increases. At present, it is impossible to determine if the intervention effect "wears off" or if other, more pervasive cultural influences come into play as the child grows.

Taken together, the data from these studies suggest that ongoing intervention (Field et al., 1980) can have a significant impact on young children born to teenagers. Once the intervention is withdrawn, however, the positive effects become less evident. The follow-up data from the Bennett and Bardon study fail to offer convincing counter evidence, since scores on the Vineland scale were based on parent reports of social maturity. These parent reports are subject to bias in favor of the intervention because treatment-group parents may have been more sensitized to the fact that their childrearing practices could affect their child's cognitive and social development. Consequently, they may have been more likely to give their child high ratings on items from the Vineland scale. While the Bennett and Bardon (1977) findings should not be disregarded, they should be viewed with caution.

The data collected to date indicate that the incidence of low birth weight and prematurity can be minimized by intervention programs for pregnant teenagers. Short-term positive effects on cognitive functions of young children have also been demonstrated in some programs, but the long-term impact on cognitive functioning and school performance remains unclear.

PREPARENT EXPERIENCES AND
THEIR IMPACT ON YOUNG ADOLESCENTS

All of the projects described to this point have focused solely on the pregnant teenager or the teenage mother. In contrast to these, there are a number of projects that have targeted their intervention for teenagers who are not yet parents or even prospective parents. Most of these "preparenting" projects are open to both male and female adolescents, and they are either part of regular educational programs in junior or senior high schools or part of a program offered by after-school youth groups, such as the Boy Scouts of America. A key feature of these projects is the combination of first-hand experiences with young children and formal instruction. Their broad aim is to provide students with experience and knowledge that will enable them to become responsible caregivers either as parents or in some occupational role of working with young children. Another feature of these preparenting projects, one which contrasts with the projects described above, is that they tend to be national in scope rather than isolated. Evaluation data regarding the impact of these projects are relatively sophisticated. In this section, the impact of three projects is examined: Project FEED (Anastasiow, 1977), Education for Parenthood (EFP) (Morris, 1977), and Exploring Childhood (von Hippel & Cohen, 1976).

While all preparenting programs combine instruction with real-world experience, they differ in terms of settings, populations served, and formats. Exploring Childhood and Project FEED were designed as in-school programs; EFP was implemented in various after-school youth organizations, such as the 4-H Clubs. As in-school programs, Project FEED was targeted for young adolescents in grades 7 and 8, and Exploring Childhood was designed primarily for high school students, although certain school districts have used the program with junior high school students. EFP has been incorporated into youth groups that serve students who are enrolled in grades 6 through 11.

Finally, the three projects differ considerably in terms of the instruction and practicum experiences they provide students. While organizations participating in the EFP project had access to the Exploring Childhood curriculum materials, they were relatively free to select the instructional format—rap sessions, lectures, role playing, and so on—that best suited their needs. Similarly, specific types of practicum experiences were selected by each organization to meet its unique objectives. Thus, in some communities participants organized programs to teach folk dancing to younger children, while participants in other communities worked as volunteers in day-care programs. The Exploring Childhood project was relatively structured in both instructional materials and types of practicum experiences. The curriculum developed for it was used in all participating schools. The practicum experiences were within ongoing educational or health care settings, although the specific practicum sites ranged from preschools to elementary schools to community health care centers. Project FEED was relatively unstructured in terms of instructional materials, although teachers were provided with suggestions and an extensive annotated list of instructional resources. Of the three projects, Project FEED was the most structured regarding practicum experiences. All participating schools provided students with practicum experiences in a preschool or day-care setting, a health care setting, and a special education setting.

EFP and Exploring Childhood have been described in more detail in Chapter 6, and Project FEED is reviewed extensively in Chapter 9; but the impression from this brief overview of the three preparenting projects is one of variations on a theme rather than of three distinctly different melodies. Similarly, their pattern of impact, discussed below, indicates a great deal of commonality among these preparenting projects.

Researchers have found that adolescents have only limited factual knowledge of child development as it relates to caring for young children (de Lissovoy, 1973; Epstein, 1979). At the same time, these adolescents often have unrealistically positive attitudes toward young children (Byles, 1975; Morris, 1977). (Data from Snyder, Eyres, and Barnard, 1979, suggest that even older women have inaccurate knowledge of child development prior to the birth of their first child.) In accordance with these findings, the developers of preparenting projects have emphasized as prime objectives the acquisition of realistic, yet positive attitudes toward young children and knowledge of developmental milestones, as well as effective child-care techniques.

The EFP project (Morris, 1977) was implemented by seven voluntary organizations in communities throughout the country. In many of these communities, pre–posttest data from both treatment and comparison groups were obtained. Using analysis of covariance procedures to adjust posttest scores for pretest differences between the two groups, the data indicate that at the end of the program, project participants knew more about young children and parenting than did comparison group adolescents. While these differences were statistically significant, the absolute differences between groups were small: out of a possible score of 52, adjusted posttest scores were 25.3 for the treatment group and 24.5 for the comparison group. Neither group was able to answer more than 50% of the items correctly, and the adjusted difference between the groups was less than 1 point. In fact, for three of the seven voluntary organizations, the adjusted posttest scores were higher for the adolescents who did not participate in the program.

Exploring Childhood (von Hippel & Cohen, 1976) has also reported data regarding knowledge gains among treatment and comparison group students. No quantitative data were provided in the evaluation summary, but there were no overall posttest differences between groups. Further analysis indicated that there were more high-scoring students in the treatment group than in the comparison group. Treatment group students scored higher on items dealing with "skills in working with children" and "ways of learning about children" than the comparison group students.

While Exploring Childhood was targeted for upper-level high school students, and EFP included adolescents ranging from grades 6 to 12, Project FEED was targeted for young adolescents in junior high or middle schools. Using a comparison group design, the data from the Project FEED evaluation (Anastasiow & Strawhun, 1977) indicate there were statistically significant differences in knowledge of child development between the groups, with project participants scoring higher than comparison group students on a post-intervention test. Project FEED participants scored higher than comparison group students at all five FEED sites with the difference being significant at three of the five sites. Across all five sites on the 64-item knowledge test,

FEED participants averaged 52% correct, while the comparison group averaged only 37% correct.

All three projects were able to demonstrate at least some differences in knowledge of young children favoring project participants over comparison group adolescents, although in some cases the data were not striking. The authors of Exploring Childhood have noted that many of the comparison group students had taken a child development course. This similarity in academic coursework may account for the lack of differences in knowledge among the groups in their evaluation. EFP is an after-school program, and perhaps there is a tendency to minimize the academic content in that setting. However, the data from Project FEED, an in-school program for students who have had no other exposure to child development, indicate that in-school instruction combined with practicum experiences can provide an appropriate context in which to introduce young adolescents to information about child development. It remains to be seen, nevertheless, if the factual knowledge adolescents gain from preparenting programs will be sufficient to meet the requirements of parenthood.

As indicated above, practicum experiences with young children comprise an important component of preparenting programs. Through real world experiences, the adolescent learns about the young child's needs and capabilities. In addition, as a consequence of successful experiences as a caregiver, the adolescent is expected to acquire realistic positive attitudes toward young children and toward caring for them. A final objective of these projects has been to improve the students' self-concept via successful practicum experiences. All three preparenting programs have collected evaluation data on attitudes toward young children and toward self.

Data from the EFP evaluation (Morris, 1977) show that adolescents entered the program with relatively positive attitudes toward young children. The degree of positiveness increased during the course of the intervention; but there was also a slight gain in positiveness among comparison group students who did not participate in the program.

In their summary of year 2 findings on the impact of the Exploring Childhood project, von Hippel and Cohen (1976) have reported that participants expressed more positive attitudes toward nonsevere punishment, dependency, and tenderness than did comparison group students. While these additional differences were noted, global attitudes toward children, adults, and self did not change as a result of participation in the project. The authors of the evaluation report note that such other variables as age, sex, ethnicity, educational ability, and previous coursework in child development were associated with student responses on the attitude measures. The authors attribute the few between-group attitude differences to the practicum experience that was provided to the project participants. While the practicum experience may have had some positive impact on attitudes, that impact was neither strong nor widely generalized.

Project FEED also assessed treatment and comparison groups on a pre-post basis in attitudes toward normal young children, handicapped young children, hospitals, and self. Analysis of covariance procedures indicated significant posttest differences in attitudes toward handicapped children and young children at three of the five sites. The attitudes of FEED participants were significantly more positive than were those of comparison group students at the end of the intervention period. An analysis of attitude toward self that combined data from all five sites also indicated significantly more positive feeling among program participants. There were some instances of significantly more positive attitudes toward hospitals among FEED participants, but these findings were not widespread (Anastasiow & Strawhun, 1977). Two months after completion of intervention, follow-up assessment of attitudes toward normal children and handicapped children was conducted with the treatment groups at two of the five sites. Results from both sites indicated that the FEED participants continued to maintain their positive attitudes toward normal and handicapped young children. At one of the sites, the students' attitudes were even more positive at the 2-month interval than they had been at the end of the intervention period. At this site, the difference in attitudes in the follow-up test versus the posttest was statistically significant. These follow-up data are similar to the reminiscence effect for learned behavior described by Hovland (1951). It suggests that the changes in attitudes that occurred among program participants were learned as a consequence of classroom and practicum experiences provided by the intervention.

With the evaluation data collected to date, the question of the value of preparenting programs can be addressed. De Lissovoy (1978) is critical of preparenting programs, as he feels the adolescent is too preoccupied with establishing his or her own identity vis-à-vis the peer group and the larger society to attend to the content of the preparenting program. One could argue, however, that the three preparenting programs described here, with their emphasis on practicum experience, provide adolescents with precisely the types of experiences they need to learn in order to be contributing members of society. This would seem an important first step toward responsible parenthood and a reasonable goal for a preparenting program for young adolescents.

An additional and potentially positive aspect of these programs is that males are included. While there are some sex differences when students enter the programs, the data indicate that both male and female adolescents make gains from preparenting training.

On the other hand, de Lissovoy's concerns about the amount of practical factual information that adolescents will retain are borne out by the data collected thus far. The national preparenting programs have operated in a wide range of settings and with a wide range of participants. In general, the evaluation data suggest that their impact has been limited, yet meaningful. Long-term follow-up studies are needed to assess how well these adolescents function once they become parents.

CONCLUSIONS AND RECOMMENDATIONS

Adolescent parenthood is a fact of life. Preparing adolescents for this role is a relatively new goal for public agencies, which is being met by a wide array of projects, ranging from preparenting practicum experience projects to postpartum mother-infant training projects. At the most general level, positive benefits have been documented for all target audiences. Still unclear are the long-term impact of these programs on the life chances of adolescents and their children and a clear-cut understanding of the optimal modes of providing intervention parenting and preparenting services to these populations. Nevertheless, the data consistently show that programs for adolescents are effective.

Long-term follow-up is crucially needed for any comprehensive evaluation of the strengths and weaknesses of these intervention programs. Persuasive arguments can be made to justify programs in that they cut down the incidence of low birth weight. If a decrease in low birth weight has only minimal long-term impact on child health or parental school success, however, it is questionable whether the programs should continue to be funded. At the same time, it is obvious that the relatively modest gains noted in most programs can be easily offset by other powerful forces, such as social isolation or poverty, which impose themselves on the adolescent mother and her child. From an overall societal perspective, it may be that under optimal conditions, decreasing the incidence of low birth weight may improve an infant's life chances, but additional, ongoing postpartum services may be needed. Negative environmental effects can minimize the impact of the original intervention.

The beneficial impact of various forms of service delivery have been reviewed in this chapter, but the research to date is insufficient for planners to make a choice among types of intervention strategies. Intervention programs work, but it remains to be determined which ones work best for whom and under what conditions. More comparative studies are needed like that carried out by Tatelbaum et al. (1978) on obstetric outcomes across health care settings. To answer questions about optimal modes of service delivery, such variables as length of the intervention program, expertise of the service provider, setting, demographic characteristics of the participants, and cost must be systematically examined.

In terms of future program evaluation, there are a number of important methodological issues to consider. Inappropriate research design may tend to minimize the probability of observing positive program effects. For example, the incidence of low birth weight nationwide is about 14.5% among adolescents (Bennett & Bardon, 1977). Thus, for 86% of teenage mothers, a nutritional intervention program will have little impact even if it is well implemented. Only by effectively matching nutritional services with those adolescents who are particularly susceptible to delivering low birth weight infants will it be possible to accurately assess the impact of an intervention program. Similarly, valid long-term follow-up studies will require thoughtful design and planning. Data should be collected only from programs that have been shown to be at least moderately effective on some short-term measure. It will do little good to conduct a follow-up study on participants in a marginally effective program.

Comprehensive baseline data are needed in many areas in order to begin a more sophisticated assessment of program impact. Populations and data collection procedures vary so much among projects that in most cases it is meaningless to try to compare the effectiveness of different programs. In a period of decreased government support for social programs, comparative data will become increasingly important.

Instrumentation also must be more closely geared to ecologically valid measures. For example, although statistically significant changes in knowledge of developmental milestones may indicate that a program is having a positive impact, the adolescent's absolute level of knowledge may still be far lower than that necessary to function as a competent parent. What do "good" parents *know* and *do* that differentiates them from "ordinary" parents? Instruments like the Caldwell HOME Inventory may be promising, but more work is needed in this area. Likewise, face validity of instructional materials and practicum experiences is no longer enough. What competencies are really needed to be an effective parent? Income level is a good predictor of both the mother's and her infant's life chances. Without accurate knowledge of crucial parenting competencies, perhaps the simplest intervention would be to provide adolescent mothers the wherewithal to maintain themselves in the middle class.

Yet another issue that has not been addressed is that of how to increase the contributive role of the father. Adolescent mothers may be unmarried, but their children are not fatherless. Projects that strive to increase the father's contribution to his child financially, emotionally, or in a caretaking capacity may have a strong positive impact on both the mother's and the child's life chances.

The works of Field et al. (1980) and Truss et al. (1977) serve as a clear warning that a one-shot program at whatever stage—preparent, prenatal, or postpartum—may not be enough. Caring for young children is complex, especially in a society where adolescent parenthood is not the norm and where supportive extended family structures are unable to compensate for the adolescent's inadequacies. The public school system may not be ideally suited to the needs of the pregnant adolescent, but effective child-care training can be provided within the school setting. Also, some projects have shown that medical and psychological services needed by the pregnant adolescent can be provided effectively within the school setting via cooperative agreements with local, medical, and social welfare agencies. Thus, if we accept that preemployment job training need not be the only function of schooling, preparenting training might be incorporated into the curriculum relatively easily.

Although the impact of any single intervention may be limited, an ongoing coordinated series of services could provide the support that male and female adolescents and their children need to overcome the negative consequences of early parenthood. The first wave of teenage parenting programs has demonstrated positive payoff. It is hoped that future programs can build upon the successful groundwork that was laid during the 1970s by those innovations.

REFERENCES

Alton, I. 1979. Nutrition services for pregnant adolescents within a public high school. Journal of the American Dietetic Association 74:667-668.

Ambrose, L. 1975. Discrimination persists against pregnant students remaining in school. Family Planning/Population Reporter 4:10-13.

Anastasiow, N. (ed.). 1977. Preventing Tomorrow's Handicapped Child Today. Institute of Child Study, Indiana University, Bloomington, Ind.

Anastasiow, N., and Strawhun, E. 1977. Evaluation procedure and results. In: N. Anastasiow (ed.), Preventing Tomorrow's Handicapped Child Today. Institute of Child Study, Indiana University, Bloomington, Ind.

Badger, E., and Burns, D. 1980. Impact of a parent education program on the personal development of teenage mothers. Journal of Pediatric Psychology 5:415-422.

Badger, E., Burns, D., and Rhoads, B. 1976. Education for adolescent mothers in a hospital setting. American Journal of Public Health 66:469-472.

Bennett, V., and Bardon, J. 1977. The effects of a school program on teenage mothers and their children. American Journal of Orthopsychiatry 47:671-678.

Berg, M., Taylor, B., Edwards, L., and Hakanson, E. 1979. Prenatal care for pregnant adolescents in a public high school. The Journal of School Health 49:32-35.

Byles, J. 1975. Teenagers' attitudes toward parenting. Health Education 6:15-18.

Cartoof, V. 1978. Postpartum services for adolescent mothers. Child Welfare 57:600-666.

de Lissovoy, V. 1973. Child care by adolescent parents. Children Today 2(4):22-25.

de Lissovoy, V. 1978. Parent education: White elephant in the classroom? Youth and Society 9:315-338.

Epstein, A. S. 1979. Pregnant teenagers' knowledge of infant development. Paper presented at the Biennial Meeting for the Society for Research in Child Development, March, San Francisco.

Field, T., Widmayer, S., Stringer, S., and Ignatoff, E. 1980. An intervention and developmental follow-up of preterm infants born to teenage, lower-class mothers. Child Development 51:426-436.

Foltz, A. M., Klerman, L. V., and Jekel, J. F. 1972. Pregnancy and special education: Who stays in school? American Journal of Public Health 62:1612-1619.

Goldstein, P., Zalar, M. K., Grady, E. W., and Smith, R. 1973. Vocational education: An unusual approach to adolescent pregnancy. The Journal of Reproductive Medicine 10:77-79.

Hovland, C. 1951. Human learning and retention. In: S. Stevens (ed.), Handbook of Experimental Psychology. Chapman and Hall, London.

Link, P. 1979. An alternative program for pregnant schoolgirls. Paper presented at the Annual International Convention, The Council for Exceptional Children (ERIC Document Reproduction Service No. ED 171 073), April, Dallas.

Morris L. (ed.). 1977. Education for Parenthood: Program, Curriculum, and Evaluation Guide. Behavior Associates, Tucson, Ariz.

Osofsky, H., and Osofsky, J. D. 1970. Adolescents as mothers: Results of a program for low income pregnant teenagers with some emphasis upon infant development. American Journal of Orthopsychiatry 40:825-834.

Robertson, E. 1978. Effect of Parent Training on Teenage Mothers. Unpublished doctoral dissertation (ERIC Document Reproduction Service No. ED 170 671), Walden University.

Sarrel, P., and Davis, C. 1966. The young unwed primipara: A study of 100 cases with 5-year follow-up. American Journal of Obstetrics and Gynecology 95:722.

Smith, P., Wait, R., Mumford, D., Nenney, S., and Hollins, B. 1978. The medical impact on an antepartum program for pregnant adolescents: A statistical analysis. American Journal of Public Health 68:169-172.

Snyder, C., Eyres, S., and Barnard, K. 1979. New findings about mothers' antenatal expectations and their relationship to infant development. American Journal of Maternal Child Nursing 4:354-357.

Stine, O., and Kelley, E. 1970. Evaluation of a school for young mothers. Pediatrics 46:581-587.

Tatelbaum, R., Adams, B., Kash, C., McAnarney, E., Roghmann, K., Coulter, M., Charney, E., and Plume, M. 1978. Management of teenage pregnancies in three different health care settings. Adolescence 13:713-728.

Truss, C., Bensen, J., Hirsh, V., and Lickiss, K. 1977. Parent training in preprimary competence. Paper presented at the Annual Convention of the American Psychological Association (ERIC Document Reproduction Service No. ED 153 701), August, San Francisco.

von Hippel, C., and Cohen, K. 1976. Summary of Evaluation Findings: Exploring Childhood: Year Two. School and Society Programs, Newton, Mass.

8

Integrating Community-Level Services for Pregnant Adolescents and Adolescent Parents

Charles Granger

ONLY RECENTLY have the problems of adolescent pregnancy and parenthood become recognized as being multifaceted and warranting multidisciplinary, coordinated prevention and treatment efforts. Bolton (1980) has suggested that "once community acceptance [of the adolescent pregnancy problem] has become a reality in the professional and private sectors, a coordinated philosophy must be developed between service providers. The programmatic availability must not be piecemeal in its approach or its timing. If an uncoordinated array of services presents ... to the adolescent, the reluctance to utilize these services will guarantee failure" (p. 229).

Consistent with this belief, that portion of Public Law 95-626 which deals with adolescent pregnancy and parenthood states that the purpose for which the government awards funds is "to establish better coordination, integration, and linkage among existing programs in order to expand and improve the availability of, and access to, needed comprehensive community services which assist in preventing unwanted initial and repeat pregnancies among adolescents, enable pregnant adolescents and adolescent parents to become productive independent contributors to family and community life, with primary emphasis on services to adolescents who are 17 years of age and under and are pregnant or who are parents'' (sec. 601, b1).

There is a great deal of intuitive appeal to the idea of the integration of services for pregnant adolescents and adolescent parents. Unfortunately, this intuitive appeal makes it easy to overlook the difficulties involved in transforming a collection of autonomously operating organizations into an integrated, cooperative unit. It becomes easy to suppose that service integration can be quickly brought about by simply meeting with representatives of various human service organizations, explaining the advantages of an integrated service approach, and securing their agreement to henceforth operate as a cooperative unit.

Past service integration efforts, however—many of which have been recounted in detail by Project Share—have shown that integrating human services is anything but simple. These projects have encountered strong resistance and complex logistical problems, have taken much longer than originally planned, and not infrequently have failed entirely.

A major premise of this chapter is that to underestimate the difficulties involved in developing integrated services is to seriously jeopardize such an effort's success. Of even more concern is the possibility that an ill-conceived and unsuccessful effort at service integration will increase resistance within a community to future service integrations. Thus, it is attempted here to describe some of the frequently encountered barriers to service integration and their causes. One hopes that this will both help provide individuals involved in future service integration with realistic expectations regarding the task and help them plan accordingly. An attempt is also made to describe those kinds of activities that appear most useful in the start-up phase of a service integration effort.

VARIETIES OF SERVICE INTEGRATION

Because service integration networks have varied so much in structure and function, a precise definition is impossible. Very generally, however, *service integration* involves an alternative mode of organizational functioning whereby once autonomous agencies interact and cooperatively deal with either administrative responsibilities or the provision of services or both. The potential advantages include the holistic treatment of clients and a decrease in service gaps and duplication. As extensive evidence for them does not exist, however, these advantages are largely hypothetical.

Structural and functional variations in existing service integration networks are surprisingly broad. Networks have been funded or unfunded, have solicited voluntary cooperation or have mandated agencies' participation, have utilized organizations whose sole purpose was to oversee the network's interactions, or have allowed participating organizations to mediate their own interactions. Clients targeted for service have been either all persons within a particular geographical area or very specific client types. Interorganizational interactions either have been administrative (e.g., joint planning, purchasing, and staff training) or have focused upon actual service provision (joint intake, diagnosis, treatment, and follow-up). Even interactions of like type have varied in frequency and intensity. Davidson (1976) has suggested that interactions have been characterized by communication, cooperation, confederation, federation, and merger. Differences among these interaction types are in terms of frequency, intensity, and formality.

Although there will be exceptions, the majority of service integration projects designed to serve pregnant adolescents and adolescent parents will be unfunded, will involve voluntary participation, and will lack the benefit of an organization whose sole function is to develop and mediate interorganizational interactions. Community-level service will probably be based on the voluntary integration model, which is the one least dependent upon legislation or higher-level funding and, therefore, the model most available to communities. It is also the most difficult type of network to establish.

DIFFICULTIES INVOLVED IN SERVICE INTEGRATION

One way to understand the difficulties of bringing about service integration is to examine the process within a planned social-change framework. Thus, service integration is considered the innovation, its proponents the change agents, and other human service organizations the potential adopters. One may then use many of the principles regarding the dissemination of innovations to make predictions about the process of developing integrated services.

Perhaps the most comprehensive review of factors associated with the dissemination of innovative programs and practices has been that provided by Rogers and Shoemaker (1971). Of particular interest here are the principles regarding rate and ease of adoption. According to these authors, the perceived attributes of innovations greatly influence their rate of adoption. Influential attributes include relative advantage, compatibility, complexity, trialability, and observability (Rogers & Shoemaker, 1971).

Relative advantage refers to the degree to which a proposed innovation is perceived to hold a significant advantage over the status quo. Such innovations will be adopted more rapidly than will those not so perceived.

Compatibility refers to the extent to which a proposed innovation is perceived to be consistent with the values, needs, and experiences of potential adopters. High compatibility tends to result in an innovation being perceived as less risky and more meaningful to potential adopters; low compatibility results in the perception of the innovation as risky and less meaningful. The rate of adoption, then, is greater in instances where compatibility is high.

Similarly, the innovation's perceived complexity, trialability, and observability are related to its rate of adoption. *Complex* innovations have potentially slower rates of adoption, due to the difficulty involved in understanding their natures and how they are used. Innovations with low *trialability*—that is, with little ability to be experimented with on a limited basis—will also be adopted more slowly. Finally, innovations with little *observability*—that is, for which results of implementation are difficult to observe—will also be adopted more slowly.

Perceived activities and attributes of change agents also affect an innovation's rate of adoption. According to Rogers and Shoemaker (1971), change agent success is positively related to the level of change agent effort. Change agents who expend a great deal of effort in dissemination are more successful than those who do not. Change agent success is also related to the degree of homophyly between change agents and other potential adopters. When change agents and adopters are similar in education, social status, values, beliefs, and so on, adoption of the innovation is more likely. When change agents and potential adopters are not thus similar, their interactions can be less productive, and innovation adoption is less likely.

When potential adopters of innovations are organizations rather than individuals, dissemination is characterized by what Rogers and Shoemaker refer to as "authority innovation decisions." The dissemination effort is complicated by the fact that within formal organizations, there are both decision and adoption units. The decision unit is an individual or group, typically in the upper levels of the bureaucratic structure, that decides whether or not to adopt the innovation. The adoption unit is an individual or group, typically in the lower levels of the bureaucratic structure, that is responsible for actually putting the innovation to use. In the process of dissemination, the decision unit becomes aware of and knowledgeable about an innovation and seeks out and interacts with its proponents. If the decision unit is persuaded to adopt the innovation, that decision is communicated downward to the adoption unit, and the action of adoption begins.

It is at the communication and action stages that difficulties arise. There is some risk that the innovation as communicated to the adoption unit by the decision unit will be dissimilar to the innovation as originally designed. Key elements may be either intentionally or unintentionally distorted or omitted. There is also some risk that the adoption unit will disagree with the adoption decision. It may not be provided with the persuasive arguments afforded the decision unit, or it may be in a position to spot flaws in the innovation that are unapparent to the decision unit. Because of its lack of organizational authority, the adoption unit may be compelled to adopt an innovation for which it has little conviction. When this occurs, the innovation's effectiveness is seriously jeopardized.

The dissemination principles and findings reviewed briefly here suggest that the process of persuading organizations to adopt a totally integrated approach will be very difficult. On a complexity-simplicity continuum, total service integration must be considered relatively complex. It calls for changed roles, responsibilities, and modes of operation. Furthermore, its relative advantage is unsubstantiated, its observability and trialability, low.

To complicate matters, change agents seldom have sufficient resources to devote to service integration development. In many cases, advocates of service integration are themselves service providers whose existing responsibilities leave little time to persuade others. Also, by the very nature of service integration development, change agents and potential adopters can be expected to have experience from different backgrounds, at least professionally; they will not completely share a professional language and will differ to some extent in terms of status, thereby complicating interactions.

Finally, because potential adopters consist of organizations, there is a good chance that difficulties will develop due to the workings of decision and adoption units. The critical features of service integration may become distorted by the time they reach adoption units, and adoption units may only half-heartedly accept or openly reject the decision to integrate services. This has been the case in many of the British Coordinating Committees (Kammerer, 1962).

Given the unsubstantiated attributes of service integration as an innovation, the necessary heterophyllous interactions, the time constraints placed on change agents, and the potential problems associated with decision and adoption units, it is not surprising that adoption of service integration projects will be slow in coming, if it comes at all.

Many of the difficulties that might be predicted on the basis of dissemination principles have been experienced by past service integration efforts. Hagebak (1979) has summarized difficulties encountered as those of barriers of organization, person, and vision.

Barriers of organization are those "clear, hard facts of organizational life based on regulation and law, funding limitations, differing agency structure and systems, and varied geographical service areas" (Hagebak, 1979, p. 576). These barriers arise from the manner in which many human services develop. Typically, when a particular human need arises or is newly perceived, special interest groups emerge and force that need into national consciousness. With increased awareness of the problem, one or more specific categorical programs are created, each with its own set of regulations, funding structures, and service areas. This piecemeal response to human need has produced the situation in which even organizations with very similar interests and goals find it difficult to work cooperatively.

Barriers of person are less tangible but certainly no less formidable. They are those behaviors commonly referred to as "turf-guarding." Individuals involved in human service delivery evidence much concern about the continued existence of their own particular organization. This concern stems in part from a genuine interest in remedying a particular human need and in part from an interest in protecting one's livelihood. Service providers have an obvious stake in protecting their organizations from "external pressures which may affect the delivery of its single service to its unique target population" (Hagebak, 1979, p. 576). The prospect of sharing its clientele and service responsibilities is construed as a threat to an organization's continued existence.

Like barriers of person, barriers of vision are intrapersonal rather than external and intangible rather than directly perceivable. *Barriers of vision,* according to Hagebak, refer to the difficulty we have in visualizing what human service delivery could be. People tend to operate human services in much the same way as they always have. Furthermore, when we propose changes, these are seldom more than variations on the existing human service theme. We just have difficulty imagining service delivery as significantly different from whatever is the status quo.

Accounts of service integration projects are replete with references to barriers of organization, person, and vision. Barriers of person and organization have been reported by Benson, Kunce, Thompson, and Allen (1973) in their description of a four-agency network in Missouri. Developing that network meant contending with pressures on agency administrators to "demonstrate the adequacy and effectiveness of the agency's established programs as a means of insuring its supply of resources" (p. 119). In addition, it meant contending with administrators' efforts to maintain a "clear-cut, uncluttered claim to a set of important activities" (p. 119).

Gans and Horton (1975) have reviewed in detail 30 service integration projects, five of which involved voluntary organizational participation (i.e., Edison Drop-Out Project, Philadelphia; Galveston Early Child Development Program, Galveston, Texas; Parent-Child Center Project, Oakland, California; Parent-Child Services Project, Portland; and the Jackson County Child Development Centers Project, Jackson County, Oregon). They found that in virtually all projects examined, the process of service integration took a good deal of time. It took time to explain what service integration meant, to secure agreement from local organizations, and to develop plans regarding the nature of linkages. Furthermore, once linkages were formed, it took time for participants to become accustomed to new modes of functioning.

In Gans and Horton's review, barriers to service integration varied to some extent, depending on characteristics of the projects themselves, with voluntary projects encountering the most barriers. The most frequent inhibitor of service integration, particularly among voluntary projects headed by service providers, was the inability to concentrate on the development of linkages, due to demands associated with existing responsibilities. When individuals already involved in human service provision take on the additional responsibilities of developing a service integration network, the demands on their time can be overwhelming.

Inhibitors encountered with almost equal frequency were those associated with the attitudes and objectives of service providers. It was not uncommon for individuals within various human service organizations to want to protect the authority of their organization. There was a tendency for service providers to want to retain the rather narrow service goals of their organization and to perceive service integration as a threat to their autonomy. This sentiment is much the same as that referred to by Hagebak's (1979) barrier of person.

Other inhibitors encountered included nonsupportive local government officials, funding guidelines that were nonsupportive of service integration, and technical and logistical problems associated with interactions among staff in different agencies in different locations. Gans and Horton concluded that, in general, local conditions could be characterized as hostile toward service integration efforts.

GENERAL STRATEGIES FOR CHANGE

The foregoing is intended, not to discourage individuals interested in human service integration, but, rather, to advise them of the difficulties involved. Human service organizations can seldom be rushed into integration, particularly when their participation is voluntary. Nor will it be easy to persuade human service agencies to adopt a totally integrated service approach. The obvious alternative is to propose the development of a select few interorganizational linkages. Using treatment linkages as an example, the road to integrated services could begin with mutual referral or mutual diagnosis. The remaining course of treatment would then be carried out individually. This scaling down of service integration should make it more trialable, more observable, less complex, less time-consuming, and less likely to meet with resistance from organizations' adopting units.

In consideration of the barriers to service integration, it appears that certain types of linkages are better suited to this start-up phase than others. A guiding principle for all network start-up activities would seem to be that threats to any individual organization's autonomy and continued existence, whether real or imagined, must be minimized.

A widely used first step during the start-up phase, and one that poses little threat, is to develop a directory of human service agencies located within a particular geographical area and which perhaps serve a particular client population. Such directories help increase service providers' awareness of other human services available locally. Agencies relevant to the concerns of this book are any that are capable of responding to the needs of pregnant adolescents or adolescent parents; this would include schools, hospitals, health clinics, employment services, day-care centers, mental health clinics, agencies that supplement income, and others. The directory could list organizations' names, addresses, phone numbers, contact persons, type of staff, and type of client served.

An activity that might be performed in conjunction with the development of a directory is the collection of information regarding existing cooperative relationships. Thus, organizations could be asked to give the names of other organizations with which they routinely interact in a cooperative manner and the nature of those interactions. It is important to specify clearly that this information will not be included in the directory but, rather, is of interest in the obtaining of a clearer picture of the way human services are delivered locally. If cooperative service delivery is found the exception rather than the rule, important evidence will have been obtained to support the case for service integration. If isolated service delivery is found the exception rather than the rule, the need for a service integration effort should be reconsidered.

Hagebak (1979) has suggested a number of activities that appear to be particularly well suited to the start-up phase, each of which "can be undertaken locally to move toward an integrated service system, on a voluntary basis, and which do no damage to the present autonomy of any participating agency" (p. 579). According to him, the process of information sharing among organizations can be an effective means not only to maximally utilize information but also to establish relationships among professionals who otherwise would seldom interact with one/each other. Information may be shared in a variety of ways. Common agency libraries can be set up; key documents produced by single organizations can be shared with other organizations; and staff members who are knowledgeable in areas of general interest can be "loaned" to other organizations.

Another strategy is to share specific short-term tasks confronted by most, if not all, human service organizations. The process of needs assessment is a good example. Representatives of participating organizations may well be able to develop a single instrument and methodology that would provide the information needed by all. The target population could then be divided in a logical manner, thereby minimizing overlap of data collected. This would not only assess needs with minimum overall effort but might also encourage interorganizational relationships of a more continuing nature.

Even closer to the ultimate integration goal is the joint case management of a particular client population. Hagebak suggests identifying a client population with a need for a variety of services. Clearly, pregnant adolescents and adolescent parents fit this requirement. An interagency team can then be developed to respond to the needs of that particular type of client and jointly work on identification, assessment, development of a treatment plan, treatment itself, and follow-up. Once again, there is little threat to the autonomy of an individual organization, since only a specific client type is involved. Also, there is ample opportunity for each organization to assess the value of cooperative interorganizational functioning from its own perspective.

Of Hagebak's suggested start-up activities, closest to the integration ideal is the creation of joint outreach sites. These are likely to be highly conducive to service integration but also likely to be very difficult to accomplish. Outreach sites, because of their typically smaller size and less permanent nature, may be much easier to co-locate. The idea of shared overhead costs alone may make outreach site co-location sufficiently attractive for organizations to warrant a trial effort. In such a situation, nontask- as well as task-related interpersonal relationships can develop and form the basis for integrated service delivery.

The advisability of a gradual approach, beginning with linkages that pose little threat to individual organizations' autonomy, is borne out by the experiences of the service integration projects reviewed by Gans and Horton (1975). These local-level projects, considered generally successful, were all still developing linkages after a year of work. No project had developed a majority of the possible linkage types outlined by the authors. Of even more interest, it was found that different types of linkages required different periods of time to develop. Those that developed the most rapidly were also those that posed the least threat to an organization's autonomy. This was particularly true for projects characterized by voluntary participation. The joint training of staff, purchase of services, and outstationing of staff were more quickly brought about than were joint budgeting, joint planning, or joint record-keeping.

SUMMARY

This chapter has attempted to present the developing of service integration as an achievable, but complicated, undertaking. Working against it are its innovative nature as a service mode as well as the interpersonal phenomena encountered when dissemination takes place within organizations. These barriers have proved formidable. Given the difficulties, general guidelines and a few specific activities have been recommended as useful in initiating a service integration effort. Particular attention has been paid to efforts in which participation is voluntary and in which proponents are already involved in the provision of services. It has also been recommended that proposed interactions consist of a scaled-down version of a totally integrated service network and that those link-ups that are initially proposed be of the sort that minimize threats to participants' autonomy.

Even though service integration is much more difficult to accomplish than is generally perceived, it holds promise for the more efficient and effective treatment of such clients as pregnant adolescents and adolescent parents. Certainly, the multifaceted and grave needs of that population warrant the effort required to develop integrated services.

REFERENCES

Benson, J. K., Kunce, J. T., Thompson, C. A., and Allen, D. L. 1973. Coordinating Human Services: A Sociological Study of an Interorganizational Network. Regional Rehabilitation Research Institute, University of Missouri, Columbia, Mo.

Bolton, F. G. 1980. The Pregnant Adolescent: Problems of Premature Parenthood. Sage Publications, Beverly Hills, Calif.

Davidson, S. M. 1976. Planning and coordination of social services in multiorganizational contexts. Social Service Review March:115–137.

Gans, S. P., and Horton, G. T. 1975. Integration of Human Services: The State and Municipal Levels. Prager Publishers, New York.

Hagebak, B. R. 1979. Local human service delivery: The integration imperative. Public Administration Review. November/December:575–582.

Kammerer, G. M. 1962. British and American Child Welfare Services: A Comparative Study in Administration. Wayne State University Press, Detroit.

Public Law 95-626. United States Statutes at Large, 1978. Vol. 92.

Rogers, E. M., and Shoemaker, F. F. 1971. Communication of Innovations. The Free Press, New York.

Service Integration Methodology. 1979. Project Share Bibliography Series, Rockville, Md.

9

How FEED Operates in Different Communities

Cindy Carlson

People, although similar in many ways, differ in size, shape, age, taste, resources, and life-style. It comes as no surprise that even a relatively simple aspect of life, like the selection of clothing, is governed by a wide range of variables. One variable in the selection of clothing, however—the fit—stands out as critical. Clothing that does not fit comfortably will not be purchased, will be altered to fit, or, if purchased and discovered to be uncomfortable, will be discarded. Rather than alter clothing, persons may alter some aspect of themselves, such as weight, to permit the desired clothing to fit. As is well known, this change is less likely, unless motivated by more than one article of clothing. Ideally, a person could have all clothing tailor-made; realistically, the cost is prohibitive and the expertise, limited.

Communities, agencies, and school systems, like people, differ in size, shape, complexity, complexion, and resources. Like persons wanting well-fitted clothing, communities want well-fitted programs. Few communities or school systems can afford to develop from scratch a program to meet every need. Few communities fit the ideal specifications of predesigned programs. Indeed, they are unlikely to change significantly to accommodate a new program. Consequently, flexibility and adaptability are key characteristics that enhance the successful adoption and maintenance of any parenting program. Either a parenting program will be adaptable to local needs and resources or it will be rejected. Research has uniformly concluded that program adoption does not occur without program adaptation (Emrick & Peterson, 1978; Larsen & Agarwala-Rogers, 1977).

While program adaptation is essential for program adoption, the alteration of program design risks the loss of program integrity—that unique constellation of components that permits promised outcomes to be attained. The alteration of a parenting program that is not designed to "flex" to local needs may result in decreased program effectiveness. In parenting program selection and adaptation, therefore, it is important for communities to be aware of 1) the unique characteristics and needs of their community or school, 2) those characteristics and components of the parenting program that address identified needs, and 3) the flexibility of (1) and (2) to "fit." The Facilitative Environments Encouraging Development (FEED) program, or Project FEED (1981), provides an example of a parenting program that is designed to adapt to the school and community in which it is implemented and yet attain stated goals. The following section examines Project FEED and the flexibility of its components in adapting to local needs.

FACILITATIVE ENVIRONMENTS
ENCOURAGING DEVELOPMENT (FEED)

Project FEED is an educational program designed to provide young people with knowledge of child development and skills in child care gained from positive caregiving experiences with normal and handicapped infants and children. The goals of the FEED program are multiple and designed to change not only knowledge but also attitudes and behavior. To accomplish stated goals, 33 objectives have been offered for possible inclusion in a FEED curriculum, with four core objectives designated as essential (Table 1). FEED objectives are accomplished through a combination of traditional classroom experience with three types of experiential learning in 1) a normal preschool setting, 2) a handicapped setting, and 3) a medical or health-related setting. FEED core objectives and the general structure for achieving stated goals remain constant. What, where, to whom, and how FEED is taught varies, however, with the structure, resources, and identified needs of the school and surrounding community.

What to Teach?

What is taught in a FEED program is adaptable to the needs of the school and community. School personnel implementing a FEED program are provided with a *Curriculum Guide* (Project FEED, 1981), which contains a list of objectives plus supporting material, such as sample lesson plans, bibliography of existing resources, and information on how to secure teaching aids. FEED staff select the objectives that are most suitable to the needs of the adolescents in that particular school or community.

In one large metropolitan school district, for example, health board statistics reveal a high incidence of infant mortality relative to national statistics. FEED teachers in this school district consequently might choose curriculum objectives that cover such relevant topics as probable causes of premature birth, preventive measures that help maintain good health, and infant and premature baby procedures in hospitals (Project FEED, 1981). In contrast, FEED teachers in a school with an established vocational exploration program supported by community volunteer and babysitting opportunities might choose the curriculum objectives of demonstrating proficiency in the basic care procedures for infants, toddlers, and preschool children or in the planning and preparing of nutritious snacks for children ages 0–5 (Project FEED, 1981).

Additional factors influencing the FEED curriculum are the content area in which the course is included, the interests and competencies of the teacher, and the course duration. FEED is designed to combine with any ongoing subject in the school, such as home economics, science, social studies, vocational education, or health. Who teaches FEED is determined primarily by factors of interest, availability, and ability. Project FEED recommends that parent education teachers have knowledge of child development. Child development cuts across multiple disciplines and is a common requirement for teacher certification. Consequently, teachers can be selected from a variety of subject areas. The teacher who has recently become a parent may have the greatest competence and interest in good parenting, regardless of subject certification. The content area in which FEED is embedded, however, undoubtedly flavors the curriculum. Course duration also influences the breadth or depth of curriculum. Middle schools vary considerably in course length and scheduling, which, in turn, places structural limits on curriculum comprehensiveness. The *Curriculum Guide* (Project FEED, 1981) provides sample curriculums for 9-, 16-, and 36-week programs.

Where to Teach?

Project FEED, as previously discussed, is designed to be implemented in a school curriculum and to utilize local agencies to accomplish objectives. It recommends three types of practicum settings for an optimal program—a preschool, a handicapped setting, and a health care setting.

Selected practicum sites should reflect the agencies that the adolescent taking the FEED course would typically use as a young parent or child-care worker. In a large urban area, for example, the health care facility typically selected as the FEED health care practicum site would be a neighborhood health clinic. In a rural area, where neither a hospital nor a health clinic exists in close proximity, FEED students accompany a visiting public health nurse.

Such variations in practicum settings are logical for both the handicapped and the normal preschool experience, reflecting the resources of the local community. A large metropolitan area may have as many as 20 different

Table 1. Project FEED student objectives

Objectives are to enable participating students to:	Classroom	Practicum	Hospital
*1. Specify general developmental patterns of children ages 0 to 5: a. Physical b. Social c. Emotional d. Cognitive e. Language	1	2	3
*2. Specify major handicapping conditions of young children who have or are: a. Physical handicaps b. Cerebral palsy c. Hard of hearing d. Partially sighted/blind e. Minimal brain dysfunction f. Behaviorally/emotionally disturbed g. Speech or language impaired h. Mentally handicapped i. Multiply handicapped	1	2	3
3. Specify similarities and differences between "normal" and "special needs" children	1	2	3
4. Describe the behavior of individual children with whom they are working	2	1	3
5. Specify and explain reasons for preschool regulations and routines	2	1	3
6. Explain the value of play for children ages 0 to 5 in stimulating growth in the following areas: a. Physical b. Social c. Emotional d. Cognitive e. Language	1	2	3
7. Explain how play materials in the practicum setting aid in a child's development	3	2	3

Item			
*8. Explain how an adult can interact with a child to stimulate growth in the following areas: a. Physical d. Cognitive b. Social e. Language c. Emotional	1	2	3
9. Specify inside and outside environments that stimulate growth in the following areas: a. Physical d. Cognitive b. Social e. Language c. Emotional	1	2	3
*10. Devise activities appropriate for the developmental level of the children with whom they are working	2	1	3
11. Devise activities that stimulate growth and development of children with special needs	3	1	3
12. List specific strategies for assisting children with special needs in reaching developmental goals	2	1	3
13. Interact comfortably with children in their practicum settings	3	1	3
14. Interact with each child in ways that will stimulate the child's individual growth pattern	3	1	3
15. Compare various child guidance methods in terms of their appropriateness for children ages 0 to 5	1	2	3
16. Use discipline measures that reflect understanding of the developmental level of the children	3	1	3
17. Demonstrate proficiency in the following care procedures of infants, toddlers, and preschool children: a. Responding to distress calls in a positive manner b. Approaching with tolerance "learning situations," such as toilet training and dressing	1	1	2

continued

Table 1. (continued)

Objectives are to enable participating students to:	Classroom	Practicum	Hospital
17. (continued) Demonstrate proficiency in care procedures			
c. Defining safe play environments for different developmental levels			
d. Diapering			
e. Feeding procedures for children at different developmental levels			
18. Specify effects of adequate diet on the following developmental areas:	1	2	2
a. Physical c. Emotional			
b. Social d. Cognitive			
19. Plan and prepare nutritious snacks and lunches for children ages 0 to 5	2	1	3
20. Specify similarities and differences in the following family lifestyles:	1	3	3
a. Extended c. Single-parent			
b. Nuclear d. Communal			
21. Specify similarities and differences in family lifestyles of different cultures	1	3	3
22. Specify major purposes of local service agencies available to individuals and families	1	2	2
23. Identify local community facilities available to normal and handicapped preschool children	1	2	3
24. Specify some preventive measures that help to maintain good health	2	3	1
25. Identify major health care facilities in their neighborhood or community	2	3	1
26. Specify regular and emergency procedures of neighborhood and community health care facilities	3	3	1
27. Specify major responsibilities of professionals and paraprofessionals in hospitals, health care-related facilities, and preschool programs	3	1	1

28. Specify and explain reasons for hospital regulations and routines	2	3	1
29. Specify probable causes of premature birth	3	3	1
30. Describe infant care procedures in a hospital	3	3	1
31. Describe premature baby care procedures in a hospital	3	3	1
32. Specify some gross and/or early symptoms of the following common childhood diseases, illnesses, or accidents:	2	3	1

a. Colds and chest and upper respiratory infections
b. Chicken pox
c. Mumps
d. Measles (different kinds)
e. Concussions
f. Diabetes
g. Scarlet fever
h. Body shock
i. Poisoning

33. Demonstrate emergency procedures to cope with the following illnesses and accidents of young children until medical help arrives:	2	3	1

a. High fevers
b. Chills
c. Concussions
d. Suspected bone breakage
e. Suspected internal injury
f. Poisoning
g. Shock
h. Heavy bleeding
i. Heavy chest/upper respiratory congestion
j. Superficial bleeding from abrasions/cuts
k. Swelling from bumps to the head

Source: Curriculum Guide, Project FEED, Educational Development Center, 55 Chapel St., Newton, Mass. 02160.
*Core curriculum objective.

1 = major emphasis; 2 = some emphasis; 3 = little or no emphasis.

preschool facilities within proximity to the FEED classroom. On the other hand, a rural area having no organized preschool may arrange for FEED students to have field experiences in homes with the mothers of toddlers.

Handicapped settings can be readily found in middle to large urban areas. In rural areas, however, experiences with handicapped children are often found only within the school system, and experiences with severely disturbed children may require field trips to more specialized facilities. Consequently, FEED programs vary in the setting used to meet curriculum objectives and depend upon the availability of resources within the community.

Whom to Teach?

It is the expressed premise of the FEED program that since few persons live their lives devoid of encounters with children, all teenagers would benefit from exposure to information about child development and care. This view is shared by T. H. Bell, United States Commissioner of Education, 1974–1976, who stated, "Nothing is more important to our society than to prepare teenage boys and girls to become effective parents" (*The Fine Art of Parenting*, 1977). Based on recent national statistics indicating higher birthrates for younger adolescents, Project FEED was designed and targeted for middle-school-age students (Project FEED, 1981). While parenting education in schools remains atypical, courses that do exist are most often electives at the high school level and most frequently attended by girls. Yet, recent literature has indicated that fathers play a critical parent role in the development of children and that this role differs from that of the mother (Lamb, 1979). Consequently, all FEED projects include both males and females.

A second consideration of school systems preparing to implement parenting education programs, such as FEED, is: At what age is it most appropriate to teach child development to teenagers? While national birthrate statistics suggest that the middle school period is not too early, the following considerations may guide the decision: How many teenage girls become pregnant each year? What is their average age? Has the average age changed over time? What is the most common outcome of teenage pregnancy in the community? How many teenagers are responsible or would like to assume responsibility for the care of children? At what grade do students begin career exploration?

The FEED program has been taught to students ranging from grades 6 to 10. Flexibility of student grade and age is possible with FEED, due to its provision of a bibliography of teaching resources, rather than a set of required curricula. Community needs should determine the grade level at which parenting education is begun; student characteristics, such as reading level and interest, should influence the selection of curriculum materials.

Parent education, particularly such a program as FEED, which includes the invaluable experiential component, can be perceived as stretching the already limited resources of a school system, resulting in the selection of a more limited population for parenting education. Possible responses to resource constraints may be the identification of a high-risk adolescent population, the offering of parenting education to a particularly interested population, or the systematic evaluation of parent education program variations.

Once again, the concept operates of "fit" between school-population needs and school-community resources. One school within a system may have a particularly high rate of adolescent pregnancy and births that results in a parenting education course requirement for all students. Proximate field sites may permit the inclusion of an experiential component at minimal expenditure. Another school within the system may have a low incidence of teenage pregnancy but a strongly supported career program; an elective child-care course may be appropriate within such a setting. FEED operates within school systems as both a required course and an elective. Data have not yet been collected to measure the differences, if any, in outcomes attained in these differing situations.

How Does It Fit Together?

How the instruction base, curriculum content, selected field sites, participating students, personnel, and allocation of resources all fit together provides another source of variation in FEED programs. Two determinants of the organization of any program are 1) the structural characteristics of the setting and 2) the resources available.

Structural characteristics of middle schools, such as operating time, duration of class periods, modular versus rigid scheduling, curriculum flexibility, and size, influence the operation and organization of a field-based parenting education program such as FEED. FEED successfully operates 1) as an intensive 3-hour-per-day, 2-week minicourse in a career exploration program or 2) for an entire year with 1 hour weekly of classroom instruction and 2 hours weekly of practicum experience. Most typically, FEED programs operate as semester-long classes that meet for 2-hour blocks three times per week.

The organization of a field-based parenting program is constrained not only by the structure and schedule of the school but also by the structure and schedule of the participating field sites. At certain times of the day—for example, nap time at the preschool—there may be little activity at the field site that is of value to the accomplishment of stated course objectives. Participating field sites may also be unable to accommodate the typical number of students in a classroom. Flexible scheduling of FEED students into various field sites would then be required.

Resources, the second major determinant of the organization of a parenting program such as FEED, include curriculum materials, transportation, and the number, type, and time of paid staff. The resources allocated to a FEED program are usually determined by the amount of them available, plus the commitment of persons in control of their allocation.

FEED projects have operated at minimum cost, with resource allocation limited to one class period of instruction by a teacher already hired by the school system. Such a limited allocation of resources is possible in a setting where field experiences are so proximate as to eliminate transportation costs and where the number of participating students and field sites is small enough to require only minimal uncompensated coordinating time of the teacher. Programs operating on extremely restricted budgets can obtain a variety of useful child-care and parenting materials without charge from government agencies and child-oriented industries.

In contrast, the resource allocation of a parenting program with committed financial support utilizes multiple field sites and serves several hundred adolescents annually but requires a part-time paid coordinator, several teachers, a teacher's aide, and an extensive curriculum library.

Each FEED program represents a unique constellation of organization, personnel, curriculum, resources, settings, and population variables. No one FEED program is identical to another but, rather, represents a unique match between the flexibility of the program and the environment in which it is situated. To help clarify the range of possible FEED variations, several program examples are provided.

A SIMPLE SURBURBAN PROGRAM

The organization of this kind of program is influenced by the setting characteristics of a rigid class schedule, the availability of field sites that can accommodate large numbers of students, the lack of proximate field sites, and small school size. This program example is labeled ''simple'' because the field site schedule is fairly uncomplicated. In this sample school district, the simple surburban FEED program is a required course for 7th graders within the home economics department. The district has two elementary schools, which extend to the 8th grade. Approximately 80 students are enrolled in each grade.

The FEED program in this school system meets three times per week for a 2-hour block. One FEED class with approximately 35 students is conducted by one teacher in each semester. Students meet as a group for one class period. Then, one-half of each class goes to field placement in one of the two remaining class periods. Field sites consist of a major hospital, a developmental training center serving the state region, and a city-sponsored preschool program.

Several factors influenced the organization of this program. First, the rigid class scheduling of the school required an adjustment to accommodate an experiential program. Students could not attend field sites within the 50-minute-per-class format. This required the cooperation of another staff person to teach a 2-hour class on alternate days. Another scheduling change was made to reduce transportation costs. FEED programs were scheduled during the first 2 periods in one school and in the second two periods in the other school to permit one bus and bus driver to accomplish transportation requirements.

The scheduling of the schools and the need for transportation to field placements can be considered a program constraint. However, the availability within the adjacent metropolitan area of field sites of size and complexity adequate to accommodate a maximum of 20 students per visit simplifies the curriculum planning and scheduling demands of the program.

The emphasis of this FEED curriculum, based upon the expressed needs of the community, is the care of young children, career exploration, and the effects of alcohol, smoking, and drug abuse on child development.

CONTRASTING URBAN PROGRAMS

The following two examples of urban FEED programs are similar in that both are elective courses for 8th grade students operating in junior high schools and both require no transportation costs. However, the programs provide an interesting contrast in field site complexity and resource allocation.

Urban Program No. 1 is characterized by the number of field experiences available to students and by a high level of resource allocation. Two FEED programs operate within this school, accommodating approximately 100 students. The FEED class meets for 1 hour per week for classroom instruction and for 2 hours per week for field experience for the entire school year. The school is operated on a modular schedule, which permits individual students to be at various field sites at different times. Practicum sites consist of one major hospital, several specialized facilities for handicapped children, and up to 20 normal preschool centers. No more than two to three FEED students visit each site at the same time. As this is in a major urban area, students are accustomed to traveling by bus or subway and, consequently, use these modes of transportation to attend field placements.

The FEED program in Urban Program No. 1 is taught by the social studies department and rotated among several teachers each year. A part-time Project FEED coordinator is paid to coordinate field site schedules with student schedules, to serve as a communication liaison between the multiple field sites and the classroom teachers, and to assist teachers in keeping up to date on new curriculum materials. The duration of the FEED class, plus the availability of a paid coordinator at Program No. 1, permits all objectives to be covered in the curriculum.

Urban Program No. 2 provides a contrast in resource allocation and field site utilization. Urban Program No. 2 consists of an educational campus comprising an elementary school; a preschool; several handicapped programs, including an infant stimulation program; a junior high school; and an adjacent neighborhood health clinic. The unique concentration of resources in this program permits program operation without transportation costs. In addition, the FEED program in Urban Program No. 2 has used numerous government agencies and industrial headquarters in order to obtain free curriculum materials—an additional cost cutter.

The FEED program in Urban Program No. 2 consists of an elective health class that meets daily for one class period over an 8-week grading period. Students meet for classroom instruction on Monday of each week, attend field placements in triads on Tuesday through Thursday, and rejoin for class discussion on Friday. The class is team taught, permitting one of the two teachers to plan curriculum while the other visits field sites to evaluate student performance. In response to both the placement of the course within the field of health and a high rate of teenage pregnancy and premature births within this urban area, the curriculum content of the FEED program emphasizes health-related issues regarding pregnancy, birth, the infant, and the adolescent.

A RURAL PROGRAM

The sample rural FEED program provides an example of adapting to limited community resources while maintaining high quality. It is conducted in a small high school's 9th-grade science class. The science class meets for an entire year, the FEED program being one 9-week component of the curriculum. One teacher is in charge of both the class and the FEED program. Staff roles are flexible within the small school setting, which permits assistance, if needed, from the principal, office staff, or other teachers in conducting the program.

The limited organized facilities in this rural community encourage imaginative use of local resources to meet the experiential components of the FEED program. Health objectives are accomplished by having FEED students accompany a visiting public health nurse and attend a weekly well-baby clinic. Normal preschool experiences are obtained through a single Head Start program and augmented by visits to the home of volunteer mothers with infants and/or toddlers. Handicapped children are bussed to a neighboring school district for specialized services. Consequently, the handicapped experience is accomplished through field trips to a larger metropolitan area.

The science class is scheduled back-to-back with a study hall, to permit field site visits twice a week, with the student foregoing study hall during that 9-week period. Parental consent is obtained for this alteration in the schedule. Transportation is loosely organized through a combination of school bus service, parent drivers, and walking. The Parent-Teacher Association raises funds for the field trips. Falling within the science class, the FEED curriculum is oriented toward health, child development, and medicine.

PROBLEMS OF ADOPTION, IMPLEMENTATION, AND MAINTENANCE

As can be imagined from the variability of programs and environments described, the successful "fitting" of an experiential parenting education program to relatively inflexible school and community structures with limited resources and competing demands is a challenging, creative, and time-consuming task that requires the energies of one or more highly motivated persons. Specifically addressing the implementation of innovative programs in the schools, House (1974) has noted that given the flat reward structure, the energy output required is seldom worthwhile for school personnel. The problem of obtaining the commitment and energies of school personnel to implement a parenting program is compounded by the consensus of research that program adoption in schools is primarily through social and political networks (Emrick & Peterson, 1978). Consequently, the process of parenting program adoption, implementation, and maintenance is variable, unreliable, and dependent upon the role of the school system and the personality qualities of its personnel. The adoption of new programs is predictable in only two aspects: 1) the process is lengthy and 2) personal intervention, generally by an outside consultant, is necessary (Emrick & Peterson, 1978; Fairweather, Sanders, Tornatsky, & Harris, 1974). In sum, a unique mix of persons and situations permits the fitting together of the essential roles, resources, power linkages, and communications that will permit the adoption and implementation of the innovative parenting education program.

The experience of Project FEED has indicated that the successful adoption and implementation of an experiential parent education program depends on the combined forces of key internal contact persons at different administrative levels, plus the external support of a consultant. An advocate team consisting of a central administrator, a school principal, and an energetic classroom teacher is essential. An individual at any of the three levels might be persuaded to adopt the FEED program but could not implement it successfully without the cooperation of the other two. In addition, without the support of an external consultant, persuasion of all levels of personnel is unlikely to result in implementation.

House (1974) has clarified the pattern of FEED adoption. According to House, the power to initiate an innovation within the relatively static social structure of the school typically resides with an administrator or member of the central administrative staff, because these roles permit the highest level of intra- and extrasystem communication. Mobility and career orientation are factors that increase an administrator's receptivity to innovation. A school principal interested in adopting FEED is likely to have become a principal recently and/or to perceive the role as one of several career steps. Implementation of FEED is perceived as a means of achieving social centrality and prestige within the school system. The entrance of a new principal also serves to "unfreeze" the structure, thus facilitating the adoption of a new program.

The support of a school principal is necessary—but seldom adequate—for the successful implementation of any innovative program. While the classroom teacher lacks the resources to initiate a parenting program, he or she almost always determines whether or not, and to what degree or for how long, implementation will occur. Factors influencing the teacher's decision are recognition by the principal, availability of release time to work on the innovation, and recommendation of the innovation by a fellow, usually "well-acquainted" teacher (House, 1974). All of these factors were found to be important in the successful implementation and maintenance of the FEED program.

The utilization of resources outside the individual school for the experiential component of Project FEED usually requires the support of a central administrative staff person. If this is not the case in the initial adoption and implementation, it is always so for the maintenance of the program. Successful implementation never occurs from the central administration downward (as might be expected). Thus, Fairweather et al. (1974) have found that high status and power are not predictive of adoption. Rather, adoption requires the initiative of lower-status persons who are willing to work actively for the innovation long enough to assure its implementation.

Given a motivated, mutually supportive, and multilevel advocate group for implementation of the innovative FEED program, the support of the external consultant is important. In the program, a field coordinator presents information to interested persons as well as makes efforts to reach potentially interested audiences. Expressions of interest are followed up by mailed descriptive information and telephone calls, in order to clarify program goals, assess needs, and establish essential personal contact. Continued interest is encouraged through a site visit to several administrative levels to broaden the base of support and to establish a commitment to action through the planning of a training workshop. Additional follow-up telephone calls and occasionally another site visit are necessary to maintain the momentum from training to actual implementation. Maintenance is encouraged by supporting the school system's moves to institutionalize the program, providing resource aid when possible, informing participants through a newsletter of their membership in a greater network, and reinforcing key individuals by personal telephone contacts.

Fairweather et al. (1974) revealed two broad stages in the adoption and implementation of an innovation, each supported by different variables: 1) a cognitive stage, which includes awareness of need, accumulation of knowledge, and formation of a positive attitude, and 2) a performance stage, which includes behaviors that activate adoption. According to Fairweather et al., it is the movement from stage 1 to stage 2 that requires the active, personal, and frequent communication of an external consultant who acts as a catalyst for moving from positive intention to action.

SUMMARY

The expansion of opportunities within communities for parenting education among adolescents may be crucial to the future of society. The success of parenting education programs depends upon obtaining a good fit between characteristics of the program and those of the school or community that supports the program. These programs must be able to adapt to environmental constraints and to utilize environmental assets while at the same time maintaining adequate program integrity to accomplish desired outcomes.

Project FEED demonstrates the attempt of one parenting education program to build in the flexibility and inflexibility necessary to obtain desired goals within various school and community settings. The programs described above suggest the range of resource utilization possible at the same time that essential characteristics are maintained.

While the need for information among adolescents about the care of infants and children becomes more and more accepted, the implementation of parent education in schools—particularly in times of fiscal restraint—remains innovative and controversial. Therefore, the adoption, implementation, and maintenance of parenthood education within the schools or agencies of a community require the continuous energy, commitment, and vigilance of persons at a variety of administrative and/or power levels. Bureaucratic institutionalization and the development of broad-based support provides insurance against the elimination of newly established programs.

REFERENCES

Emrick J. A., and Peterson, S. M. 1978. A Synthesis of Findings Across Five Recent Studies of Educational Dissemination and Change. Educational Knowledge Dissemination and Utilization Occasional Paper Series, Far West Laboratory for Educational Research and Development, San Francisco.

Fairweather, G. W., Sanders, D. H., Tornatsky, L. G., and Harris, R. N., Jr. 1974. Creating Change in Mental Health Organizations. Pergamon Press, New York.

House, E. R. 1974. The Politics of Educational Innovation. McCutchan Publishing Corporation, Berkeley, Calif.

Lamb, M. E. 1979. Parental influence and the father's role. American Psychologist 34:938–943.

Larsen, J. K., and Agarwala-Rogers, R. 1977. Re-Invention of innovation ideas: Modified? Adopted? None of the Above? Evaluation 4:136–140.

Project FEED (Facilitative Environments Encouraging Development). 1981. Developed by the Institute for Child Study, Indiana University, Bloomington, Ind. (Materials now distributed by Educational Development Center, 55 Chapel Street, Newton, Mass. 02160.)

The Fine Art of Parenting. 1977. Brochure distributed by the National Parent-Teacher Association and the National March of Dimes, Chicago.

10

The Problem Recognized

Solutions in Dispute

Nicholas J. Anastasiow

TEENAGE PREGNANCIES continue to increase, as reflected in the title of the most recent Planned Parenthood Publication: "The Problem That Hasn't Gone Away" (Alan Guttmacher Institute, 1981). A recent article in the *Rocky Mountain News* has presented an accurate description of the current situation in many large urban areas in the United States and, one might assume, many urban areas of the world:

Preteens' Sex Lives Worry D.C. Social Workers

The sex lives of many of Washington's preteen and teenage children have become increasingly active, according to city records and health and social workers.

But experts interviewed by *The Washington Post* say that children's sexual activity in Washington seems to mirror that of children around the nation.

For example, records on abortions, births, venereal diseases and interviews show that:

- Nearly 200 14-year-olds in Washington had babies between 1977 and 1980. Fourteen of those young mothers were giving birth to their second child.
- The number of children per 100,000 in the 14-or-younger age bracket who were treated for gonorrhea was six times higher in Washington than in the nation as a whole in 1980.
- About 400 abortions were performed on girls 14 or younger, according to statistics in 1979, the last year for which records are available.

"I think we have seen recently an increase [in early teen-age sex] and younger ages—as young as 10," said Alicia Fairley, acting chief of social services in the District of Columbia Department of Human Services.

"We see that increasing. It's not dramatic, but it's significant enough to cause concerns."

"Twelve used to be a pretty good cut-off age [as the youngest age of sexual activity]. But now we're seeing it drop."

Marilyn Bowie, executive director of the District of Columbia Interagency Council on Family Planning, agrees that there seems to be more young people engaging in sexual activity at an earlier age.

Based on recent studies, she said, "There is no reason whatever to think that Washington would be radically different from the nation as a whole" ("Preteens' Sex Lives," 1981).

SOLUTIONS IN DISPUTE

Although there is much sound and fury over the problem, there are major efforts to block any attempt to provide teenagers with information about sex. James J. Kilpatrick, nationally syndicated columnist of a conservative stance, has recently attacked another conservative, Senator Orrin Hatch and the legislation he has introduced in Congress (Kilpatrick, 1981). The legislation introduced would attempt to promote sexual abstinence before marriage, encourage family interaction with their teens, and provide teaching materials for the schools. Kilpatrick decries that any "true" conservative would sponsor a federally funded program to prepare teaching materials. Senator Hatch comes from Utah, where the Morman Church has encouraged its members to establish a family night in which all members of the family are to stay home and interact with each other. The Morman Church and leaders of the Catholic Church are strong advocates of the position that sex education is the province of the family. The Morman Church appears to be more active than the Catholic Church in encouraging families to teach their children about the responsibilities of childrearing and childbearing.

Senator Jeremiah Denton, co-author of the bill with Senator Hatch, stresses that the bill's intent is to have young unmarried women put their babies up for adoption and to prohibit government sponsoring of Planned Parenthood or of any information on sex education and abortion. Denton believes the solution is to help religious organizations and voluntary associations to "promote self-discipline and chastity" among the young (Kilpatrick, 1981).

The Center for Population Options has noted that currently there are in the United States several groups of "morality vigilantes" who want to discourage the teaching of sex education in school. The Center for Population Options' stance is that

... everyone has the right to make informed choices about sex and parenthood. But no one has valid options without pertinent information, available family-planning services, and the resources to use those services.

Today, it is the adolescents who suffer most from the limitation of their choices. The Center for Population Options, therefore, concentrates on bringing teenagers information about *what* their options are, *why* their choices are important, and *how* they can responsibly exercise their reproductive options (Center for Population Options, 1980).

At the same time, the Moral Majority is bringing increasing pressure on television producers to reduce the number of programs dealing with problems of unwanted pregnancies, as well as sexual themes in general, and on advertisers in the mass media to eliminate sexual undercurrents in their ads. The pressure from the Moral Majority is two-pronged, as it attempts to deny information at both ends of the continuum. At one end, it stands with a large group of liberals who suggest that sex innuendoes in advertising may be a factor in encouraging sexual intercourse among the very young. Frequently attacked is a full-page ad for blue jeans in which a young female movie star, bare to the waist, is astride a young attractive male, also bare to the waist, with both rears featured prominently.

Another example the liberal and conservative factions cite as contributing to teenage sex is Paul Anka singing: "You're having my baby. What a wonderful way to say you love me." Both groups perceive the song as having a contributing effect to teenage pregnancies. While the liberals would not directly prohibit that the song be produced, they would encourage its discontinuance.

At the other end of the continuum, the liberal position objects to any mandatory censorship, and thus its advocates are left with counterattack, through program information, as their means of addressing the problem. A series of spot commercials that deals directly with the teenage pregnancy issue has been initiated featuring well-known artists. The artists state some hard facts. For example, "A child is not a piece of clothing. If the style changes, you can't get rid of it" (Stevens, 1981). In essence, the liberal group tries to make information available in direct facts rather than in veiled euphemisms. Other examples include the statements by rock star Janis Ian, "To have a kid in order to leave home is out of the frying pan and into the fire" and by country singer Charlie Daniels, "It takes a lot of time to raise a child. It's not a damn automobile, something you can take home, and try it, and if you don't like it, take it back."

Thus, although several national spokesmen for liberal, conservative, and rightist groups have addressed the problem of teenage pregnancy, their solutions vary as to what role the federal government and schools should play in attempting a solution. The liberals would provide a range of information, whereas the moderate conservatives would not accept federally funded education programs. An emerging conservative group would provide information to encourage chastity, and the ultraconservative group would ban all information. Clearly, living in a pluralistic society makes it difficult to come to terms with issues that are there defined in terms of morality rather than biology.

Abortion is a major political issue, with the right-to-life groups as strongly against all abortion as the proabortion groups are for the right to choose abortion. What is common between both factions, as Dempsey (1981) has noted, is their distaste for abortion. For the woman undergoing abortion, it is a traumatic experience, particularly for the preteen and teen. Janus (1981) has presented some poignant and disturbing case studies of interviews of adolescents who had undergone abortion. As stated earlier, abortion is not a solution to the issue of unwanted pregnancy; it is a means to terminate pregnancy. The legal issues involved are not the central theme of this book. The reader is referred to Dempsey (1981) for a discussion of the current issues and numbers of abortions by state and their costs to the state in terms of dollars. Janus (1981) has discussed the human cost of abortion.

There is a growing concern by professionals in law, medicine, social work, and psychology about the problems of the adolescent, how adolescent pregnancy is perceived, and many current related issues. Preteen and teenage runaways number in the millions, with many of these young people becoming prostitutes. Teen alcoholism, smoking, and drug use continue at high levels. Suicide rivals accidents as the cause of teen deaths.

Psychologists, such as Janus (1981), look to the eroding structure of the family as contributing to the breakdown of traditional mores and values of the Judeo-Christian culture once dominant in the United States. Janus is concerned with a growing "anything goes" attitude within the culture and the continued emphasis on sex in the mass media, which, he believes, contributes to a breakdown of the nuclear family structure and the role it plays in holding the fabric of society together. Janus tends to lump women's liberation and the sexual revolution as the major causes of increased sexuality—a position one may question. As noted earlier in this book, a sexual revolution occurred in the United States in the 1920s, and the increase in percentage, by age group, of teenagers who engage in sex before 18 is a straight-line increase from that decade to this one. The destruction of the structure of the family is complex, and simplistic analyses attributing the decline to single movements will not suffice.

Dempsey (1981) has presented an overview of current efforts to establish national policy on how to strengthen and aid the family. He summarizes the activities, goals, and accomplishments of the White House Conference on Families and the workshops conducted within the framework of that conference. An appendix to his book includes the 60 recommendations from the conference. These recommendations range from concerns about the family's economic status to the family's responsibilities.

As Dempsey (1981) has noted, there is confusion as to whether the family is the problem—or the solution to the problem:

> If it [the family] is the problem, we need to expand our treatment service systems; if it is the solution, we need to support its efforts to be self-sufficient in satisfying its needs—not only for safety and security and problem solving but for self-actualization. If it is both, we need a balanced mixed strategy" (pp. 132–133).

Many professionals are opting for a ''both'' position and are suggesting that efforts need to be conducted at the state, rather than the national, level.

The National Association of State Boards of Education (Alexander, 1980, 1981) has suggested a state-level approach to the problem of adolescent sexuality, pregnancy, and parenthood. Its suggested list of policies covers development of interagency coordination, capacity, staffing, and delivery of services. The policies recommend the provision of a wide array of health services and specify services to be provided by state educational agencies:

> The state education agency shall encourage local education agencies to develop and/or maintain special services to meet the comprehensive education needs of pregnant adolescents, their partners, and adolescent parents. The state agency shall provide technical assistance to local agencies in the development of comprehensive instructional programs and educational services for the target population.

> The state education agency shall encourage the local education agencies to provide career awareness education and counseling, including job skills training, job counseling/career exploration, and job referral/placement opportunities as part of the comprehensive services for pregnant adolescents/adolescent parents, to assist them in achieving economic self-support and personal self-sufficiency.

> The state education agency shall require that decisions regarding whether to remain in regular school or to transfer to an alternative educational program be made by the student. The student shall be encouraged to involve her family in making this decision. A physician's recommendation should be considered when appropriate. The state agency shall review the local education agencies' practices to assure that pregnant adolescent/adolescent parents are being provided the same educational and extra-curricular opportunities as other students.

> The state education agency shall require the local education agencies to encourage adolescents to continue in school during pregnancy and to return to school after delivery. The local agencies should seek out adolescent parents who have withdrawn and encourage them to return to school. Counseling should be provided to assist adolescent parents in returning to or staying in school.

> The state education agency shall adopt a sequential curriculum for family life and parenthood education, including human sexuality, which may be required of/adopted by the local education agencies. The state education agency shall involve representatives from the local level and professionals from other fields in the development of this curriculum. The curriculum shall begin as early as possible, tailored to the developmental level of the students involved, and shall be reviewed regularly by appropriate groups. It shall be available to all students; however, parents shall be allowed to excuse their child(ren) from this instruction.

> Training and certification in this area shall be required for all family life and parenthood education instructors. The state education agency shall ensure that adequate training is available.

> To assist adults in their role as parents, the state education agency shall encourage local education agencies to promote and assist in the development of

parenthood education in or out of school settings, to provide all parents with information about child development, and to assist parents in understanding the special needs of their child(ren). The state education agency shall encourage the development of parenthood education programs through the elementary/secondary schools or through other community institutions, such as community schools, adult education programs, parent-teacher-student associations, churches, civic groups, health clinics, social service agencies, and community colleges.

(Alexander, 1981, pp. 49–50)

IN THE MEANTIME

Throughout this book, the authors have stressed the need to teach child development and the responsibilities of childrearing and care. Although sex education need not be an issue when such an approach is taken, and although Chapter 4 provided glimpses of alternative emphases, nevertheless, most adolescent programs do stress sex education. Project FEED is but one example of what can happen in communities that wish to provide young people with accurate information on how children grow and develop and on their responsibility as potential parents to facilitate the process. More accurate assessment of children's development enables parents to more adequately facilitate their infants' growth. A recent study by Granger (1981) has suggested that this may be a major contribution of the FEED program. In his study of adolescents' expectations of infants' development, FEED students' expectations were found uniformly more accurate than those of non-FEED students.

The "FEED" title is double-edged: Facilitative Environments Encouraging Development refers, on the one hand, to the environment parents provide for their infants and children to maintain healthy development. On the other hand, it refers to the environments schools can provide for their students. In numerous ways, students and education and health care professionals have testified to or demonstrated the impact the FEED practicum experiences have had on students' lives.

A superintendent of a school district in which a FEED program operates notes:

> We have in this program done something that I think's very essential to public school programs, and certainly something we have not done enough of—and that is involve many other agencies in the community.
>
> I think the four walls and the text book no longer suffice for a child's education. So we like for our programs, to the extent possible, to get out and be a part of the community, and the FEED program has certainly involved a number of community agencies. It's been a community effort, really.
>
> One of the greatest strengths, I think, of this program, has been the fact that youngsters involved are having a hands-on experience.

So, if anyone were to ask me, is FEED something worthwhile to consider in our school program, you know, if a colleague of mine, a superintendent in a neighboring district for example, were to ask me, I'd have to say by all means, yes. I think it's one of the finest programs we have instituted in the school system. It's not a paper and pencil thing, but it's good for kids (*Kids Are People Too*, 1981, Educational Development Center, Newton, Mass.).

A teacher in the same district talks about the impact of FEED on her students:

Part of our plan for doing FEED is the improvement in self-concept among our teenagers. So many of them, even those who are excellent in school and good academics, don't have a very good self-image. I have found that as long as I've been teaching in junior high and middle school that that's about as low an ebb that self-image sinks to, at 12 and 13 to 14 years old. Teenagers don't get a lot of positive reinforcement, that is there is not a lot of opportunity for adults to say to them, that's good . . . I like what you do . . . you're a good person, and you're a productive person, and you're efficient, and I need you. They don't get those messages very often, and in this program they get them a lot (*Kids Are People Too*, 1981, Educational Development Center, Newton, Mass.).

A school counselor states:

In working with 8th graders, I sit down with them in small groups, and we talk about things that they're involved with in school and at home.
And we are trying to work with these students from the aspect of success. Because I think success breeds success, and I say to them, you know, what is it in school that you like. Why do you like to get up and come to school . . . some of them will say, gee, you know, I really don't like it. I come because I have to, but then they start thinking about it and, I say, well then, pick one thing that you really like more than the others. And some of them, invariably, it comes up, the FEED project . . . the FEED program.
It's getting out and being exposed to people and being able to teach them something. It makes, you know, in a teacher's term, I guess that it enhances their self-concept, that it makes them feel better as human beings because they can work with somebody who looks up to them and thinks they're great. And it just improves their outlook, totally. And it not only improves their outlook in that program, but I think it carries over to other classes.
For some kids it's the only reason they come to school. For others, it just makes the school experience a lot better (*Kids Are People Too*, 1981, Educational Development Center, Newton, Mass.).

As many authors have noted, middle adolescence is a bleak period (Lipsitz, 1977), and providing meaningful practicum experiences can have great impact on the lives of these students. Several states have initiated out-of-school vocational programs (for a list of such programs write to Conference on Youth Participation, U.S. Department of Education, 19th and Stout St., Denver, Colorado) that claim successes similar to what has been noted with FEED—enthusiastic response on the part of the adolescent to being meaningfully engaged in useful work.

The means and the tools are available to make life more fulfilling for the preteen and teen in today's society. The solution is economically feasible and does not require vast expenditures for buildings and equipment. What it does require is a willingness on the part of community agencies to cooperate in assuming responsibility for assisting our young people toward adult maturity.

It requires caring about children and the children they will have—more than about protecting the organizations that have been developed to train them. It requires greater flexibility in school organization than is currently demonstrated by the schools. It can be done. It must be done. The alternative is to continue to have millions of young people living in daily chaos and desperation.

ACKNOWLEDGMENT

Project FEED was supported by a grant from the Bureau for the Education of the Handicapped, OEO-0-74-2417.

REFERENCES

Alan Guttmacher Institute. 1981. The Problem That Hasn't Gone Away. Alan Guttmacher Institute, New York.

Alexander, S. J. 1980. Overview of State Policies Related to Adolescent Parenthood: A Report of the Adolescent Parenthood Project. National Association of State Boards of Education, Washington, D.C.

Alexander, S. J. 1981. Suggested Services and Policies Related to Adolescent Parenthood. National Association of State Boards of Education, 444 N. Capital St., N.W., Suite 526, Washington, D.C., pp. 49–50.

Center for Population Options. 1980. Options. A publication of the Center for Population Options, Summer, Washington, D.C.

Dempsey, J. J. 1981. The Family and Public Policy: The Issue of the 1980s. Paul H. Brookes Publishing Co., Baltimore.

Granger, C. R. 1981. Young adolescents' knowledge of child development. Unpublished doctoral dissertation, Indiana University, Bloomington, Ind.

Janus, S. 1981. The Death of Innocence. William Morrow and Company, Inc., New York.

Kids Are People Too. 1981. Educational Development Center, 55 Chapel Street, Newton, Mass. 02160.

Kilpatrick, J. Conservatives and teen-age sex. Rocky Mountain News, July 17, 1981, p. 73.

Lipsitz, J. 1977. Growing Up Forgotten. Lexington Books, Lexington, Maine.

Preteens' sex lives worry D.C. social workers. Rocky Mountain News, July 19, 1981, p. 36.

Stevens, J. Teens: The rock project. Washington Post, May 26, 1981, B5.

Index